Bow Street Beak

Ronald Bartle

With a Foreword by Lord Hurd

≋ WATERSIDE PRESS

Bow Street Beak
Ronald Bartle

ISBN 978-1-909976-36-8 (Paperback)
ISBN 978-1-910979-20-4 (Epub ebook)
ISBN 978-1-910979-21-1 (Adobe ebook)

Copyright © 2000, 2016 This work is the copyright of Ronald Bartle. All intellectual property and associated rights are hereby asserted and reserved by her in full compliance with UK, European and international law. No part of this book may be copied, reproduced, stored in any retrieval system or transmitted in any form or by any means, or in any language, including in hard copy or via the internet, without the prior written permission of the publishers to whom all such rights have been assigned worldwide.

Cover design © 2016 Waterside Press.

Main UK distributor Gardners Books, 1 Whittle Drive, Eastbourne, East Sussex, BN23 6QH. Tel: +44 (0)1323 521777; sales@gardners.com; www.gardners.com

North American distribution Ingram Book Company, One Ingram Blvd, La Vergne, TN 37086, USA. Tel: (+1) 615 793 5000; inquiry@ingramcontent.com

Cataloguing-In-Publication Data A catalogue record for this book can be obtained from the British Library.

Printed by Lightning Source.

e-book *Bow Street Beak* is available as an ebook and also to subscribers of Myilibrary, Dawsonera, ebrary, and Ebscohost.

This Revised Edition Published 2016 by
Waterside Press
Sherfield Gables
Sherfield-on-Loddon
Hook, Hampshire
United Kingdom RG27 0JG

Telephone +44(0)1256 882250
E-mail enquiries@watersidepress.co.uk
Online catalogue WatersidePress.co.uk

"Why Sir," said Johnson, "I suppose this must be the law since you have been told so in Bow Street."

Boswell's Life of Dr Johnson

Table of Contents

First edition *vi*
About the author *vii*
Acknowledgements *viii*
Foreword *ix*

    Introduction 11

1 **Drama at the Palace** 17
    The Queen's Intruder *17*
    Descent from Above *23*
    A Short Postscript *24*

2 **Laughter in Court** 25
    The Walter Mitty Complex *27*
    Anyone Fancy a Pigeon? *28*
    A Wild Goose Chase *29*
    What a Charmer! *30*
    When is a Square not a Square? *31*
    Do You Like Your Cockroach Grilled or Boiled? *33*
    A Flutter in the Dove-Cote *34*
    …And Tears *36*

3 **Coping with Crime** 39
    Sentencing the Violent Offender *46*
    The Sex Offender *49*
    Sentencing the Minor Drug Offender *52*

4 **Policemen Under Fire** 59
    The Wapping Riots *59*
    The Guildford Four Police Officers *63*

5	Security—Does it Exist?	79
6	**Crime Knows No Frontiers**	83
7	**Magistrates: Lay and Stipendiary**	93
8	**These I Have Known**	105
9	**A Day in the Life of a London Magistrate**	115
10	**A Little of Myself**	131
	Making Justice More Efficient *140*	
11	**Japanese Days**	153
	Nagasaki *160*	
12	**The Pinochet Drama**	165
13	**Summing It Up**	181

Appendix *185*

Index *187*

First edition

Bow Street Beak was first published by Barry Rose in 2000 and this revised edition is reproduced by kind permission of his daughter Diana.

About the author

Ronald Bartle was Deputy Chief Stipendiary Magistrate (now District Judge) for Inner London. His books include *The Telephone Murder: The Mysterious Death of Julia Wallace* (2012); *The Police Witness: A Guide to Presenting Evidence in Court* (1984 onwards) and *Three Cases that Shook the Law* (2016).

Acknowledgements

To the memory of the late Barry Rose MBE and to Miss Diana Rose who has kindly agreed to this book being republished, and with thanks to my wife Molly whose enthusiasm and support enabled this to take place.

Foreword

I have known since Cambridge days that Ron Bartle possesses lively views and a stylish pen. He has turned both to good account in these reflections on his life as a Bow Street Beak.

A huge amount is written about crime, criminals and sentencing. We have the television soap operas. We have the tedious debate, which Ron Bartle rightly criticises, between the political parties about who is tough and who is soft on crime. We have learned academic volumes on criminology. But alongside these there is scope for a practical account based on down-to-earth experience of how the system actually works — particularly when this can be laced with humour and many proofs of the eccentricity of human nature. You do not need to agree with all Ron Bartle's conclusions to be stimulated as well as entertained by the story of a vivid career.

The Rt Hon Lord Hurd of Westwell CH, CBE, PC
October 1999

Bow Street Beak

Introduction

It it good to be able to revisit this book, written over 15 years ago. A great deal has changed in that time and a certain nostalgia is added to by the fact that Bow Street Magistrates' Court no longer exists and so there will be no more "Bow Street beaks." Neither do stipendiary magistrates as such, who are now known by the perhaps more grand sounding title of district judge as I explain in the closing chapters. Even the Lord Chancellor's Department has become the Ministry of Justice (after a brief spell as the Department for Constitutional Affairs). And the legal landscape has changed: in terms of procedure, substantive law (including the creation of new offences) and the availability (or lack) of legal aid to defend cases or put forward mitigation. The Criminal Justice Act 2003 in particular made many changes including in order to incorporate some of the suggestions I made in the original version and that are noted later in the book. In a more streamlined age it may also be that there is less scope for "characters" of the kind I describe in the book, from within the system or without, even if they make life interesting. Just occasionally and where I think it is useful to the reader I have added notes about some changes.

The book is about my work and not about myself since the former is, I trust, of some interest to the reader whilst the latter I may confidently assume is of none. It concerns the 20 years during which I sat on the bench at Bow Street Court as a Metropolitan Stipendiary Magistrate dispensing justice, or what I hope and trust has been justice, to a variety of offenders, many of them minor and some quite major, who passed through the dock day-after-day, year-after-year.

The jurisdiction of Bow Street Court broadly speaking covered that area of London known as the West End. It belonged to the South Westminster Division of Inner London, the court-house being situated in Covent Garden opposite the Royal Opera House. It is said that when Queen

Victoria went to the opera she found the view of Bow Street so uncongenial that she directed the curtains of her hansom cab to be drawn on that side. The name of the court derived from the design of the street which is shaped somewhat like an archer's bow.

The significance of this particular court was not derived from the central position which it occupied. The reason why it was universally acknowledged to be the "flagship" magistrates' court, not only of London but also of England, is twofold. First, it was traditionally the court at which the Chief Magistrate resided. Secondly, it enjoyed a special jurisdiction in the form of extradition. This meant that Bow Street stipendiary magistrates were specially designated by statute and with the Lord Chancellor's approval, to hear applications by foreign states for the return of offenders who were fugitives from justice in those countries.

I am not intending to dwell on the early history of Bow Street Court or to describe the celebrated cases which took place there during the eighteenth and nineteenth centuries. It would seem appropriate, however, that by way of introduction I should touch quite briefly upon this subject.

The story begins when, in the year 1740, a Colonel Thomas de Veil, a justice of the peace for the counties of Middlesex and Westminster, moved his magistrate's office from a house in Soho to a house in Bow Street. From such apparently innocuous origins there began a process by which the administration and enforcement of summary criminal justice slowly spread across London and, in due course, throughout the country as a whole. De Veil launched this historic development but of far greater importance was the work done by his immediate successors Henry and John Fielding and Saunders Welch.

Henry Fielding had already achieved fame as an author, *Tom Jones* being his masterpiece, but he was far too active a man to rest upon his literary laurels. He set about his new profession as a magistrate with great enthusiasm and resolve.

At the request of the government he drew up a plan to combat the criminals who infested the streets of London. He also engaged a small number of volunteer "policemen", thus laying the foundations for the famous Bow Street Runners, a body of independent law enforcers whose courage and devotion to duty was to win for them an international reputation. In these days when our newspapers and television screens contain so much reporting of crime it is some consolation to bear in mind that compared with the London of the eighteenth century, the capital city of today is a relatively secure and orderly place. The absence of a police force and of a developed system of criminal courts greatly contributed to the inadequacy of such meagre forces of law and order which did exist, confronted as they were by a degree of violence, thieving and mayhem unimaginable today. This was illustrated to the full by the Gordon Riots in which the mob indulged in an orgy of destruction for days on end until the military finally gained control. A great debt is due to Henry Fielding for his efforts to confront London's criminals, but the work he began was carried crucially forward by his half-brother John and John's assistant and subsequent successor Saunders Welch.

Sir John Fielding and Saunders Welch laid the basis for the administration of magisterial justice in London and established a routine of court sittings at Bow Street. Most importantly, however, Fielding and Welch introduced the then revolutionary principle that magistrates should be both qualified lawyers *and* paid for their services. This had the dual effect of marking the end of those "trading" justices, who were not averse to accepting bribes, while also ensuring that judgment was in the hands of trained lawyers. It also introduced the concept of a body of full-time, salaried and pensionable stipendiary magistrates which later made such an important impact on the metropolis and some of the larger provincial towns and cities. John Fielding established another important precedent when, somewhat surprisingly as the result of his own suggestion, he received a knighthood which became a traditional honour, with a very few exceptions, for all succeeding Chief Metropolitan Magistrates.

Fielding's letter in this matter to the Duke of Newcastle makes interesting reading. It is dated December 12, 1757:

"My Lord,

As the subject of the following letter is of the most delicate nature it requires more than candour; nay it stands in need even of the partiality of a friend, not to read it to the disadvantage of the author; but having experienced both to a high degree in Your Grace, I have ventured, without reserve, to expose it to your perusal. Indeed I cannot avoid being conscious that soliciting honours is the poorest evidence of deserving them; and when I consider how greatly I have been supported by Your Grace, and how universally, among the best of people, my conduct, as a magistrate, has been approved, I think my ambition ought to retire and contentedly feast on self-approbation.

And I likewise know that a perseverance in integrity and an impartial administration of justice will ever secure to me that invaluable reward, the esteem of the praiseworthy. But as this activity in my office which has procured me these acceptable advantages has at the same time rendered me obnoxious to many bodies of people, who have been the objects of justice and whose wicked and oppressive designs have been by my vigilance obstructed (viz sharpers and gamesters of all kinds, and all the publicans within the Bills of Mortality, on account of the Bill I drew against cheats and for punishing gaming in public houses which passed last Sessions. Secondly, the pawnbrokers: having laid them likewise under some restrictions. Thirdly, those bodies of journey-men of almost every trade whose combinations I have been industrious to break by the vigorous execution of penal laws, and lastly the malice of thieves and robbers) I think that if His Majesty would be graciously pleased to confer the same honour on me as he did on Sir Thomas Duveil, it would greatly conduce to my own safety, strengthen my power and add much to my influence. And as it would be a public testimony of being protected and approved by my Royal Master, it would prevent mob insolence and facilitate the execution of any future plan I might be so happy to contrive for the public good.

I am confident that I am not in the least anxious for the increase of power to abuse it; nor is what I ask unprecedented however it may be undeserved; and I frankly own that my wishes to be still more useful, joined to the strong desire I have of receiving this mark of His Majesty's approbation is the true motive of troubling Your Grace with this letter; the purport of which I must submit to your kind consideration and am resolved to rest satisfied with the event.

I am, with the highest respect My Lord, Your Grace's most dutiful and the public's faithful servant.

J. Fielding."

Four years later Fielding's wish was granted. The letter which brought this about is one of the most important documents in the history of Bow Street. It impresses, first, for the fine eighteenth century Johnsonian prose—a sad reminder that the age when a letter was a literary product is indeed past. Secondly, the shrewdness of the phraseology is remarkable. There is nothing grovelling or subservient about the approach. Indeed, Fielding does not conceal for a moment his pride in his own achievements up to that date. It is a simple request supported by logical argument. Nevertheless, the acquisition of a formidable honour on the basis of one's own recommendation, rather than that of others, must have been as unlikely in the eighteenth century as it most assuredly would be today!

The Metropolitan Police Courts Act of 1839 established the position of Chief Metropolitan Magistrate and introduced the power to appoint 27 stipendiaries. This proposal met with considerable opposition at the time and created a degree of ambivalence in the relationship between stipendiaries and lay justices which, in the view of this author, remains to the present time, a situation discussed later.

Bow Street was always recognised as the premier magistrates' court, but later changes in the organization of the Inner London somewhat modified that position. Divisionalisation concentrated the administration of the Inner London courts into various divisional boundaries. Bow Street was within the area of South Westminster, the central court of which was (and remains) Horseferry Road. Nevertheless, Bow Street retained its West End and Westminster jurisdiction and the seat of the Chief Magistrate. It also continued to exercise its powers regarding extradition. The now extinct court still I believe enjoys an imperishable place in the history of crime and punishment in this country. To have occupied a position as heir to that great history and tradition was for me been a very special privilege.

This book is neither history nor autobiography. It seeks to set out the work of the court with special reference to my own experience over 20 years, illustrated by some of the high profile cases over which it was my responsibility to preside.

I wish to conclude this Introduction to my work by saying that it has been my settled intention, in the course of my reminiscences, to omit anything which might cause pain or offence to any individual. Most of the cases over which I presided and to which I have referred occurred a considerable number of years ago and are well-documented and truthfully and accurately recorded by myself. In the main I have avoided the use of names except in those few instances which received such a degree of nationwide attention that the matter is already indelibly in the public sector.

Readers will note that in this Introduction I have frequently used the past tense, but in the text which follows I revert to that in which he original work was written. As to the quality of that text, like every author, I submit this to their judgment.

Ronald Bartle

September 2016

CHAPTER 1

Drama at the Palace

The Queen's Intruder
On July 19, 1982 it fell to me to preside at Bow Street over one of the most extraordinary cases to come before any court in English legal history. Buckingham Palace, being the principal seat of the monarch, is the most sacrosanct building in the country. Many have entered its environs when the state rooms are opened for inspection to members of the public on payment of the appropriate fee. Others are privileged to receive an invitation to one or other of the annual garden parties. A few attend investitures to receive an honour for services rendered to their nation. A very few indeed of the great and the good are invited to a private audience of Her Majesty. Michael Fagan fell into none of these categories, yet he single-handedly achieved an audience with Her Majesty in circumstances of intimacy to which neither kings, presidents nor ambassadors of great nations could hope to attain.

At the time of these remarkable events, so bizarre that a novel based upon such supposed happenings would be rejected by a publisher as too fanciful, Michael Fagan was an unemployed labourer, aged 30, of a North London working class background, whose behaviour both in court and during his brief sojourn at the palace gave rise to reasonable suspicion that he was suffering from psychological, or at least emotional problems of a fairly severe order. The story which was recounted at Bow Street and subsequently at the Old Bailey, commenced on June 7. Fagan, for reasons best known to himself, wished to meet the Queen. In furtherance of this objective at about 11.30 pm he climbed over the railings on the Buckingham Gate side of the palace and dropped into Ambassador's Court. It was then that he saw a convenient drain-pipe and, setting aside that hesitation which, as the well-known motto assures us, is the cause of lost opportunity, swiftly scaled the pipe and found himself on a flat roof. This he crossed and was then confronted by another similar means of access. In the spirit of "who dares wins," this one he also climbed.

The story at this point is taken up by Miss Sarah Jane Carter, a housemaid who, on the night in question, was sitting on her bed reading a book. The window and curtains were partly open, and on hearing a noise she turned towards the window and was shocked to see some fingers on the outside of the window, a few inches above the sill. The sight of a man's face looking through alarmed her even more and she promptly ran out of the room and recounted her experience to two other palace maids.

Meanwhile, Fagan had climbed into the room through the open window, thus inadvertently avoiding a charge of breaking and entering, and wandered into the corridors on what can only be described as a free-of-charge cultural excursion. In his own later account he declared, "I had a drop of scotch while I was there. Then there was a secretary's office. I got in and had a drop of wine. I was in there about an hour, just looking at art and taking the thing in." The wine in fact came from a bottle of Californian white which was intended by a well-wisher to add to the festivities surrounding the birth of Prince William. Fagan explained later that he was thirsty after so much climbing—an explanation which certainly has the ring of truth.

If the story so far is incredible from a security point of view what ensued is virtually unbelievable. For an hour after the alarm had been raised Fagan continued his perambulations around the palace corridors and rooms quite unmolested.

At one point he actually sat on the Throne, thus scoring another "first" in that he was the first commoner in British history to do so. Even Cromwell had declined the honour. Finally, like someone disconsolately leaving a rather boring museum, Fagan exited the palace and disappeared into the night.

One would have thought that one such amazing enterprise followed by so remarkable an escape would have satisfied anyone's taste for adventure. But not so in the case of Michael Fagan. He had taken a liking to Buckingham Palace. After all, he had not only enjoyed a tour of the art galleries free of charge, but had also received complimentary liquid refreshment into the bargain. And so he made a return visit. But this time Michael Fagan, unemployed painter and decorator and petty offender from North London, created a niche for himself in English history.

Just over a month following his first excursion he again climbed into Buckingham Palace. The fact that he was able to do so using precisely the same route is yet another comment on a security failure without parallel in the history of the British police. This time Fagan wandered along a corridor which contained the bedrooms of members of the Royal Family. Then, unabashed, he entered the Queen's bedroom and sat on her bed. Her Majesty, who had been sleeping, awoke, and with great calmness and presence of mind engaged Fagan in conversation for ten minutes. The contents of the conversation have never been revealed save that it appears that at some stage Fagan asked for a cigarette, which was not forthcoming. The most serious aspect of the encounter was the delay which occurred after the Queen had attempted to summon assistance by means of her personal alarm system. The intruder was led out of the bedroom after the timely arrival of a maidservant, and was interviewed in a palace pantry at 7.15 am by the Queen's footman, Mr Charles Whybrow, who related that Fagan was muttering, "I want to talk to the Queen, my Queen." By way of pacification he was told, "All right, but let her get dressed first."

> According to the evidence given at the Old Bailey by Mr Whybrow "The man said it was urgent and kept trying to walk past, but I stood in his way. The man's breath smelt of alcohol. I moved towards the telephone and the man looked aggressive. I decided not to alarm him. The man still seemed very tense and I said 'Would you like a drink?' Immediately he became more affable and said 'Yes please. I'll have a scotch'. I gave him a whisky."

The first policeman to arrive on the scene was Police Constable Robert Roberts. In his evidence he described Fagan as looking dirty and scruffy and smelling of whisky. Fagan told the officer that he lived at Buckingham Palace—a statement which anyone observing the ease with which he entered and left the premises might have mistaken for the truth. Other officers arrived and Fagan was taken into custody still protesting his desire to speak with Her Majesty. This event however, so far from concluding the affair, marked the start of the greatest security row involving the Royal Family during this century. This is hardly surprising. A complete stranger, of scruffy appearance and under the influence of alcohol, had penetrated the palace twice. On the first occasion he had wandered around unmolested for an hour after the alarm had been raised, and on the second had actually gained access to the Queen's bedroom. Without any doubt heads were going to roll.

Fagan was interviewed by officers at Cannon Row Police Station and was subsequently lodged in Brixton Prison's high security wing. Scotland Yard initially only provided the press with the bare facts that a man had been arrested inside the palace, that an inquiry was being held and the man was expected to be charged with burglary. When it was announced that the inquiry was at Assistant Commissioner level however, it became apparent that matters were a good deal more serious than had at first been supposed. Gradually the full scale of the incident emerged. The Commander who was in charge of uniformed officers at the palace, resigned over the security breach while the Chief Inspector in charge of the Palace Guard was transferred. The hapless Commissioner of Police, was not required to resign but took an earlier retirement than he was obliged to.

As if all this were not enough further shocks were to come. The Home Secretary at the time, Mr William Whitelaw, told a startled House of Commons that since May 1979 a number of breaches of security had occurred at the palace. On each of October 26, 1979, December 21, 1980, January 17, 1981, May 8, 1981, December 11, 1981 and January 1982 a different person had climbed over the wall or the railings and on every occasion had been detected and arrested. It is true to say that the generality of these were unduly adventurous young tourists or mentally unbalanced individuals, but this fact did nothing to allay the public disquiet. In due course, following the Assistant Commissioner's report, security arrangements at Buckingham Palace underwent a thoroughgoing revision and review.

Drama at the Palace

The case of Michael Fagan came before me at Bow Street on July 19, 1982. Never had so much publicity been generated by such a trivial charge — the theft of half a bottle of wine. The entry itself was the purely civil matter of trespass. Fagan, whose demeanour was cocky and self-confident, lounged in the dock and frequently abused his solicitor, Maurice Nadeem. The Fagan family, who were among a large crowd in the public gallery, also made frequent interjections. When the question of bail arose, Mr Fagan senior announced that he could stand bail for his son. Fagan was prompted at this point to make the extraordinary statement that his father was Rudolph Hess — not a personage whom I felt would be a satisfactory surety! Bail was objected to by the police. Detective Chief Superintendent Lloyd-Hughes said that the defendant was in a totally unpredictable state of mind and might fail to surrender, commit further offences or do an act to harm himself, since there were marks on his wrist which were said to have given rise to suspicion. Michael Fagan was committed by myself to the Central Criminal Court charged with theft of the wine together with two wholly unconnected matters: taking a Ford Cortina without the owner's consent and an assault.

The legal position regarding the entry to the palace bedroom was simply that no crime had been committed since it was merely a civil trespass. Provided there is no intent to steal, damage property or to threaten or assault the occupier at the time of entry, entering private premises is not a criminal offence as long as no damage is done when admittance is gained.

Psychiatric reports were requested but it seemed clear to me that Fagan, notwithstanding his strange behaviour, was not suffering from any identifiable mental illness.

At the Old Bailey he was found not guilty of the theft of the wine but pleaded guilty to the taking of a car. At the conclusion of the proceedings Michael Fagan's father was quoted as saying, "All this fuss over a half a bottle of wine. It costs thousands of pounds and the country's taxpayers have got to foot the bill. It should never have got this far in the first place." And nor would it have done but for the fact that the bedroom into which his son blundered was that of Her Majesty Elizabeth the Second, Queen of England.

The great public interest which attaches to Buckingham Palace provides opportunities for other, less adventurous, miscreants than those previously referred to. There are, of course, the unlicensed street photographers. I recall once, when walking along The Mall, being acknowledged by a cheery bunch of them who immediately recognised their friendly local magistrate. Among their greetings were the words: "We don't get your pay but we get the fresh air." My experience in court had taught me that the benefits of their trade went well beyond those which are conducive to good health. One of those benefits is the fact that the average tourist, when approached by a street photographer, is blissfully unaware of whether or not the photographer has been properly licensed. Another is the natural desire of all of us, when on holiday abroad, to be photographed with places of interest in the background.

My own experience of street photographers is not limited to my work on the bench. During a visit to Italy some years ago I found myself in the square in front of the Cathedral in Milan. My slightly vacant air attracted the attention of an Italian version of the gentlemen I have been describing. In no time at all I found my hands and pockets full of bird seed, whereon a swarm of pigeons descended on me in a manner reminiscent of Hitchcock's famous film *The Birds*. My abductor then took several photographs of me in quasi-Franciscan poses after which he ushered me into his office where a colleague, or I should say confederate, was waiting. The dozen or so pictures cost me the bulk of the contents of my wallet. In an attempt to salvage something from the situation I gave Bow Street as the address for postage. This must have registered because in due course they arrived. Only one is extant and that adorns the members' "funny photos" book of the Garrick Club. I have to say that since that event in my life I have been markedly less scornful of people who are, to use the colloquial term, "taken."

Another, and greatly more reprehensible group, who ply their trade in the palace environs, are the pickpockets. Distraction on the part of the victim is of the essence of the pickpocket's opportunity, and this is provided in plenty by the ceremonial occasions such as the Changing of the Guard. While the eyes of the intended target are firmly fixed on the colourful ceremonial, another, with much less interest in the ancient and historic ritual, is at work on the pockets and handbags.

A third, and somewhat pathetic class of "palace defendant" is not looking for money, but the cheapest of cheap sexual excitement. These are individuals who position themselves behind women in the crowd and push themselves against the rear quarters of the lady in question. The offence is difficult to prove, but it creates a nuisance and an embarrassment to the victim.

Descent from Above

Michael Fagan dropped into the palace from the perimeter wall. James Miller dropped in from the sky. When Miller flew up The Mall at a height of some 500 feet on course for the royal residence, landing in due course on the palace roof, he had already achieved a degree of aeronautical fame. He had crashed into the Caesar's Palace boxing ring in Las Vegas during the world heavyweight title match between Riddick Bowe and Evander Holyfield, somehow ending-up enmeshed in the ropes. He again drew attention to himself, this time in England, when he flew over Burnden Park football ground during the Bolton Wanderers versus Arsenal match. It was when he touched down at Bow Street, however, that it became my duty to bring him finally and firmly down to earth.

It was fortunate that Miller had not landed in the middle of a Royal Garden Party for he was certainly not dressed for the occasion, and the same was true of his court appearance. He presented a strange figure, even by the standards of a tribunal not unaccustomed to odd-looking individuals. Deeply tanned, he was also half naked with an open shirt that exposed a body which was bronzed and muscular without an ounce of surplus fat. He wore slippers but no socks. With his quiet, respectful manner and cropped head only the absence of a saffron robe detracted from the impression of a Buddhist monk. Yet his was a life of physical rather than spiritual adventure. As a Californian he hailed from an environment famous for its production of strange and eccentric groups and individuals. But it was the nature of the flying contraption he employed which gave me cause to reflect that James Miller was fortunate to have lived to see the inside of Court No.1 at Bow Street.

Having landed on the palace roof Miller proceeded to remove some of his clothing. There was no suggestion that this action was intended to be insulting to Her Majesty since, from his previous excellent viewpoint, he had seen that the flag on the palace roof was lowered indicating that the Queen was not in residence. He also paid a generous compliment to the Metropolitan Police expressing satisfaction at the kindly manner with which he had been treated. The weird contrivance by means of which he became airborne consisted of a propeller operated by a small and somewhat primitive engine, both of which were strapped to his back, while above him was a small parachute which enabled him to remain afloat and hopefully would break his fall in the event of engine failure, provided of course that the strands did not become entangled in the propeller. The manufacturers of such a device could not, I think, adopt the then current motto of British Airways: "We take better care of you."

Miller pleaded guilty to three breaches of aviation regulations. A charge of using threatening, abusive and insulting behaviour at the palace was dropped. In the event I decided that the nine days he had spent in police custody had grounded him for long enough. I imposed a fine of £200 and ordered his deportation. In confiscating his equipment I felt, perhaps, a trifle mean. However, I like to think that if, which I hope will be the case, James Miller lives to a ripe old age, he may one day reflect that he owes his longevity to the magistrate who separated him, all those years before, from his magnificent flying machine.

A Short Postscript

When this book was first published in 2000, I tentatively sent a copy to Buckingham Palace thereafter forgetting all about it. But a while later I was surprised to receive a reply from Queen Elizabeth II's chief correspondence officer thanking me and saying that, 'Her Majesty was interested to read your reminiscences, and has directed that the copy be held in the library at Windsor.' The letter is reproduced in full in an *Appendix* at the end of the book.

CHAPTER 2

Laughter in Court

Humour is one of the great saving factors in life. It enables us, for a short time, to forget the things that worry us—problems of health, money, relationships and so on. Humour in court relieves the predominant atmosphere of trouble and tragedy. There are, of course, some cases so grim that humour has no place, but comic relief, provided that it is spontaneous and natural and not contrived, can be like a breath of fresh air in an atmosphere heavy with solemnity.

Across the road from Bow Street Court is the famous Royal Opera House. There in the auditorium, as with theatres generally, hang two facial masks which depict both drama and real life: the sad and the happy, the one crying and the other laughing. In Bow Street Court we see both, but the emotions are real and not simulated. Humorous situations can arise in different ways. They may result from a single remark or from brief repartee between bench and Bar or bench and defendant. They can arise from the facts of the case, and occasionally the law itself presents what might be called an "A P Herbert situation."

There was a time when a great many people, a large number of them being re-offenders of the vagrant variety, were brought before the London magistrates' courts charged with being drunk in a public place. Nowadays most of these offenders are cautioned by the police unless their intoxicated condition has caused their behaviour to become a public nuisance. These are not the type of cases which one would normally expect to make the columns of the newspapers. One such, however, came before me in my early years as a stipendiary magistrate which to my amazement subsequently appeared in *Playboy* magazine of all unlikely journals. The defendant was a tall smartly dressed West Indian. He was a 40-year-old postal executive who, the day's work having been done, had decided on some liquid refreshment. Unfortunately, he refreshed himself a little too well. He was found by a keen young police constable lying face downwards on a piece of waste ground. The officer, giving his evidence, repeated the familiar formula that the defendant, after being roused, was unsteady on his feet, his speech was slurred and his eyes were glazed. At this point the defendant deftly removed his right eye which he held aloft for inspection. "Of course it looks glazed," he informed the court, "it's made of glass." The officer, although young, was already learning his trade. "Excuse me, Your Worship," he interjected, "the other one was glazed as well."

On another occasion a police inspector, together with other officers, raided a well-known East End public house where rumour had it that drinking after permitted hours was taking place. "I saw the accused standing by the bar with what appeared to be a glass of alcoholic liquid in his hand," he declared. "I pointed to the glass and said, "What are you drinking?" "He replied: 'Thanks, I'll have another light ale.'"

Another common petty offence to waste the time of the London magistrates' courts is begging. Yet it must be said that begging for money in the streets, a comparatively modern phenomenon in London, is a great public nuisance and is sometimes aggravated by aggressive conduct on the part of the beggar when his request is rejected. Generally speaking, however, if the defendant has spent a night in custody, that is considered to be sufficient penalty.

Vagrants, it seems to me, fall broadly into three main groups. There are the young people who frequently have left the parental home to enjoy greater liberty only to find themselves in the big city without employment or a roof over their heads. The adventure has turned sour, but in the main I believe it is a phase which soon passes and is outgrown. Then there are the incorrigible tramps for whom vagrancy is a way of life. They live by sleeping on park benches or under bushes, rummaging in dustbins and being fed by those organizations whose mission is to save human derelicts from going under completely. Such tramps do not wish to go into a hostel. They find the strict rules too irksome: the obligation to observe hours of entry and departure and the ban on alcohol and tobacco being brought onto the premises is a sufficient deterrent.

Finally, there is the saddest group of all. These are the mentally sick who are quite incapable of looking after themselves. They should never be on the streets at all, and it is a blot on our society that they are. The closure of institutions in which they were previously housed on the grounds of economy and the specious excuse that they are better absorbed into the community was a policy unworthy of a civilised country. Yet, with the confirmed tramp there is sometimes a strange cheerfulness. Some of the "regulars" at court are "characters." I recall one who was so fond of the court that he avoided being arrested in any jurisdiction other than our own. I remember another elderly beggar who when charged with "begging or gathering alms" insisted that it was money, not alms, that he was gathering. Another aged drunk explained his reason for striking a lady in the street: "I was so drunk I mistook her for my wife."

It will be my practice, in some of the stories which follow, to omit the proper name of the defendant. This would add nothing to the narrative and might cause embarrassment if included.

The Walter Mitty Complex

We live in times when a great many seem to believe themselves capable of doing another's job. Building societies act as banks—so for that matter do food chains and multiple stores. Banks act as building societies, and both provide legal and accountancy services. I might add to this that some civil servants who are almost entirely unfamiliar with courts devise ingenious schemes for the better administration of justice. This syndrome sometimes brings individuals into conflict with the law. I have had cases of the impersonation of police officers in which a fake "police" car has been used to stop people who are exceeding the speed limit. They have then been booked by a bogus "police officer." I have known a make-believe bishop appear in the dock and impart his blessing to all and sundry prior to departing to the catacombs below the court. One such case I especially recall is that of a young actor, I shall call Albert.

Albert had wanted to be a doctor when he left school but he lacked the qualifications for a medical institute. He therefore trained for two years as a male nurse and, commendably, worked as such at the Royal London Hospital in Whitechapel when not fulfilling acting engagements.

It was then that his imagination began to run away with him. First he put it about that he was a medical student and later on said that he had passed his final examinations. Following this he carried out a two-month term of duty as a temporary houseman. He was then offered a medical appointment. He appeared before me and pleaded guilty to dishonestly attempting to obtain the opportunity to earn remuneration as a doctor in the greater London area on or before February 25 and that on or before March 25, 1974 at the Luton and Dunstable Hospital he dishonestly obtained the opportunity to work as a doctor. There was no suggestion that any harm had been done or that Albert had received any financial advantage. I made this clear when I fined him the modest sum of £50 and gave him a conditional discharge. I also emphasised my view that his talents lay in the theatre of drama rather than medicine.

Anyone Fancy a Pigeon?

It is commonplace for a diner at one of the better London restaurants to be heard to say, when examining the menu, "I fancy a pheasant" or "I fancy a grouse." Young William fancied a pigeon. Or to be more accurate, he fancied 4,000 of them. Indeed, had he not been detected in the course of his depredations by a licensed bird-seed vendor the pigeon population of Trafalgar Square might well have been greatly depleted.

William's method of capturing the birds was simplicity itself. He would position the box, spread around some bird seed, and when the unsuspecting fowls of the air advanced on the food, assuming it to have emanated from the hand of a friendly tourist, he would pop them into the box at the rate of between 25 and 40, according to whether one accepted the account of the defendant or the witness. The fate of the birds thereafter was something over which there hung a pall of mystery, William's account was that he sold them for 20 pence each to his uncle with a view to their possible training as racing birds, but the officers of the RSPCA suspected that the well-fed pampered pigeons of Trafalgar Square might have proved to be candidates for the tables of London restaurants rather than for the rigours of competitive flying. William admitted several offences under the Wildlife and Countryside Act including having the intent to take wild birds and possessing wild birds for sale. In mitigation his solicitor advanced his client's belief that the birds were vermin, but in my view this excuse, like the captured pigeons, never got off the ground. The RSPCA inspector stated clearly, definitively and for posterity, that pigeons are not vermin. They are a pest species but are protected like other birds. Taking a dim view of William's activities I imposed a heavy fine plus costs and added a hefty bind-over to be of future good behaviour. I felt that I owed it to the tourist fraternity to ensure that he and any others similarly minded would not be a pest species in the years ahead.

A Wild Goose Chase

It occasionally happens that animals, innocent creatures of nature that they are, rocket to fame because of a kinship which they happen to enjoy with the great and the good. History abounds with examples. There was the whale which swallowed Jonah; the horse appointed a Consul by the Roman emperor Caligula; the wolf which allowed Saint Francis of Assisi to tickle its tummy and the spider whose robust efforts to build its web inspired Robert the Bruce to continue his efforts to free Scotland from the English. In this story, to which I listened with rapt attention in November 1996 the animal in question was a small brown Staffordshire bull-terrier named Buster and the great man who owned it was Mr Roy Hattersley, former deputy leader of the Labour Party. The goose had not received a name. It was one of that great throng which no man can number who depart this life unremembered and unsung. This greyleg goose was waddling in St James's Park on a bright spring morning, doubtless minding its own business, when it was spotted by Buster. Being it the Easter season, eggs were very much in vogue, but Easter, unlike Christmas, is a time when the birds which lay those eggs regard their eggs rather than themselves to be at risk. Not so on this occasion. Buster, taking advantage of the fact that his illustrious owner was dutifully complying with the law by cleaning up after his dog, broke clear of the leash and shot after the goose at a speed which would have qualified him for a race at the White City stadium. In due course the police made the gruesome discovery of the mangled body of the goose and by dint of good detective work got their man — or rather, his dog.

Naturally, as an admirer of Mr Hattersley's political oratory, I had been hoping that he would attend Bow Street and deliver an impassioned plea for his progeny worthy of Marshall Hall at his best. Instead he wrote a letter of mitigation and Buster, smugly aware that it was his owner who would have to pay the fine and not himself, proudly posed for the cameras and took his place in the pantheon of the famous dogs of history.

What a Charmer!

This is the tale, not of a dog, but of a snake. It is a common misunderstanding on the part of those persons charged with obstructing the highway, of which at Bow Street we have a great many, that provided they personally are not causing an obstruction no crime has been committed. Not so. Anyone who gathers a crowd around him or her which interferes with the free passage of pedestrians to and fro along the pavement is equally guilty of this offence. Indeed the offender does not even have to be on any part of the highway. A lady who gathered an audience by slowly removing her clothes in a room with a closed window could in addition be exposing herself to the possibility of a summons for the same reason. Covent Garden and Leicester Square are popular venues for street artists, singers, musicians and buskers of all kinds. Others may have more laudable motives. I recall a preacher who would gather his congregation by first painting an attractive picture, and then, at what he felt was an appropriate moment, Bible in hand, deliver the word. Obtaining souls by false pretences? Probably not.

Emmanuel was none of these. He was a snake charmer, but he only charmed one snake. It was indeed a very charmed, and, fortunately for Emmanuel, an apparently charming snake. With his chocolate coloured skin and grass skirt one would have assumed that Emmanuel was a recent arrival from a romantic South Sea island. In fact, disappointingly, he was a solid citizen of Hope Park, Bromley-by-Bow and the proud owner of a 17 foot python. Emmanuel appeared before me at Bow Street charged with obstructing the highway by snake-charming in a public place. At the London Zoo or Whipsnade the python would have attracted admiring glances, but when carried into Bow Street Court wrapped around the neck and shoulders of its owner the reaction of one and all was shock, alarm and distress. A horrified gaoler ordered Emmanuel to stuff the snake into a brown bag. Emmanuel assured court officials and other waiting defendants that his pet was harmless — much to the amusement of a small crowd of people at the front door of the court who were laughing at the scene, but nonetheless maintaining a healthy distance. Happily, the first creature to be mentioned in a *Bible* story was not brought into court, but I disposed of the case as quickly as possible! A court official told the press: "Animals are not allowed and we are certainly not used to dealing with snakes. We wanted it out of here as quickly as possible." Emmanuel left with his python into the human jungle that is Covent Garden.

When is a Square not a Square?

Readers of the late A P Herbert's *Misleading Cases* will recall his brilliant expositions of some of the strange situations that can, or in the realm of possibility, could arise, when the law is made to look, in the words of Mr Bumble in *Oliver Twist*, "A ass, a idiot." One is reminded of the case in which a river overflowed the adjacent road. A car travelling on the left of the road encountered a boat floating on the right hand side of the river. The question: which had the right of way? In an appeal from a decision of mine in March 1996 the question was whether or not Leicester Square could be considered enclosed premises.

Leicester Square, like Piccadilly Circus and Covent Garden, is one of the famous London landmarks which fell within my "manor" as a Bow Street Stipendiary Magistrate. Like the other two it is a favourite haunt of buskers and street entertainers of every kind, and has been for generations. Street musicians vary greatly in the service they provide for the public. Some make a moderately pleasing sound, such as student violinists supplementing their meagre grants, and the occasional harpist. Others, particularly those who perform on the underground railway, make an assault on the ear drums which could well be emulated by secret police extracting a confession from one of their victims.

Bruno was playing his guitar, a fairly benign, if commonplace instrument, in Leicester Square. The offence involved was not the sound he made but the fact that he had no licence to make it. The provisions of the London Government Act 1963 as amended by the Greater London (General Powers) Act 1984 provide for the licensing of premises used for public entertainment. The Westminster City Council, to whom I shall shortly make reference in another context, took the view that this empowered its officers to enter and search premises, namely Leicester Square and forfeit equipment belonging to Bruno. By paragraph 1(1) of Schedule 12 to the 1963 Act, "No premises shall be used for public dancing or music and any other public entertainment of the like kind, except under and in accordance with the terms of a licence…" Paragraph 1(7) of the schedule provides, "In this paragraph 'premises' includes any place." It must be said that to call the drafting of this provision sloppy would surely be an understatement, since "place" could include anything from an airport runway to the Atlantic Ocean. For the council it was accepted, however, that Schedule 12 would not cover the activities of a pied piper who moved from place-to-place. It had to be an area capable of demarcation. The council also agreed that the 1963 Act was not framed with buskers in mind.

I decided to grant Westminster City Council a warrant empowering its officers to enter and search premises at Leicester Square and forfeit equipment belonging to Bruno. A High Court judge upheld my finding but granted the defendant leave to appeal to the Court of Appeal for judicial review of my ruling. Lord Justice Sheiman, delivering the judgment of the court, said that the appeal raised questions of importance to buskers in London. He pointed out that for years the council had tolerated buskers and, if its view of the law was right, had itself been guilty of persistently breaking the law by tolerating buskers on its land. It was surely apparent that the defendant did not have Leicester Square to himself. Moreover, said the court, it was artificial for the council to use its powers to serve a warrant to obtain a right of entry to a place in its own ownership, and for which it had no need of any warrant. The situation was not one to which Schedule 12 applied. The defendant won his appeal.

Do You Like Your Cockroach Grilled or Boiled?

Food hygiene is not in itself a proper subject for jest. It is a vital factor in the area of public health. The degree of concern to which this subject gives rise has been witnessed in crises over first eggs and then beef, the latter resulting in thousands of cattle being slaughtered. Those whose responsibility it is to enforce the law which imposes penalties for unclean kitchens and other such places where food is stored, processed and prepared have a clear duty to do so. That is the bottom line on this particular topic. That having been said, it sometimes seems to this author, and here I express a purely personal view, that the authorities can at times be a little over-zealous.

In 1983 the Westminster City Council, through their environmental health officers, were conducting a series of inspections, or more colloquially, a blitz, of London restaurants, clubs, hotels and such like places where food is served, with the wholly meritorious object of ensuring that the kitchens of these establishments were free from dirt and infestation. Some of the establishments in question bear famous names. One such being Brooks's Club of St James. Brooks's is an ancient and distinguished gentleman's club which boasts among its former members a dozen prime ministers together with many other figures of fame and prestige.

The Westminster City Council brought 30 summonses alleging contravention of food and hygiene regulations and two under the health and safety at work laws. The club pleaded guilty to four of the food and hygiene regulations and the two health and safety summonses. The remainder were contested. The club had been visited on a spot check without prior notice at lunch time when the kitchens were at their busiest. The main subject of complaint, the presence of mouse droppings and cockroach infestation, was clearly a serious allegation, and, if substantiated, represented a very real health hazard. To read the reports in the press at the time, however, one would have thought that the little creatures outnumbered the members by thousands to one. "Hundreds and thousands of mouse droppings and cockroach remains" were the descriptions of the kitchens which appeared in several newspapers. It seemed to me that many of the council's complaints, such as spots of grease on the ceiling, unwashed crockery and cutlery and matters of that kind lacked substance since at the busiest time of the day these things may sometimes be found in the best of kitchens.

Evidence was given on behalf of the club that the kitchen floor was cleaned three or four times a day and that the building was closed twice a year to allow outside contractors to clean the cooking area. "We have very high standards of cleanliness," said the head chef. Consequently I dismissed 20 of the summonses. Having done so the next question for my consideration was that of costs. This was an important issue since I had dismissed the majority of the summonses, and although costs normally follow the event, I felt that they should be reduced appropriately. In so doing I commented on the fact that although, subsequent to the first visit by the inspector the club had spent £40,000 putting right the matters complained of, the summonses were served nonetheless. It seemed to me that it was open to the council to exercise their discretion and refrain, on that basis, from further proceedings. I also commented that it would be wrong to make an example of a famous institution for that reason alone if a prosecution could be avoided on the grounds that all the faults had been rectified. These remarks sparked an angry reaction from the Westminster City Council. A letter of complaint was written to the Lord Chancellor saying that my observations were unjustified and inappropriate and concluding with an expression of concern that "… if Mr Bartle holds the view which he apparently has expressed and if any of these cases are listed before him, he may not come to them with the necessary objectivity."

I am glad to say that the complaint was rejected and my reputation for impartiality remained unsullied. The cartoonist, Jak, in his inimitable style, provided an epitaph of the case. Two members of Brooks's, one young and the other elderly, were admiring two portraits of the Victorian era. The caption read: "Willoughby got eaten by cannibals in Africa and there wasn't much left of Snodgrass after the cockroaches had finished with him!"

A Flutter in the Dove-Cote

I hope that I am not a puritan, whatever that word may mean. I do, however, believe, and always have believed, that gambling in all its diverse forms ranks high on the list of human follies. My considered view of gambling as a source of income is that those who cannot afford it ought not to and those who can afford it don't need to. Those who take advantage of this craving do all in their power to give it an air of respectability. This is invariably the case when money is being made by exploiting human weakness. Gambling dens are termed "sporting clubs" and gamblers are called "punters" or even "patrons." Engaging in a game of chance is "playing." I have been to the Derby once in my life and was thoroughly bored by the entire proceedings. I have visited the delightful principality of Monaco on holiday a number of times and greatly enjoyed it. On two occasions only, from a sense of curiosity, I have entered the casino in Monte Carlo. My reaction has been wonder at how otherwise intelligent people could wish to hand over their earnings to croupiers. Far better to give the money to charity than pay the taxes which would otherwise have to be met by the good folk of that charming place. However, these are personal opinions and had no relevance whatever to a case I tried in which I learnt more about gaming and the law appertaining thereto than I had previously been aware of during my lifetime. In the result I was cast in the wholly unsought after role of the bookies' friend, although I should add that this situation did not result in my receiving any useful "tips."

Camelot, a body which needs no further introduction, brought three summonses under the Lotteries and Amusements Act 1976 against William Hill (London) Ltd, Coral Racing Ltd and Ladbrooke Racing (Central London) Ltd alleging a breach by each of the defendants respectively on April 17, 1997 of section 2(1)(b) of that Act.

The case concerned the game of chance operated by the defendants, known as forty nines and the question at issue was whether this game consisted of a lottery, in which case it would be unlawful, or whether it amounted to fixed odds betting which the defendants were licensed to conduct. There were no significant differences between the prosecution and the defence as to the facts and it was agreed that much the same system of play was operated by each of the defendants. Forty nines is a game of pure chance. From 49 coloured and numbered balls a draw takes place from which six are selected. The numbers are communicated to bookmakers and fixed odds are placed on numbers one to five. Punters complete a slip. In order to win it is necessary to guess correctly one or more of the numbers selected. The odds become more favourable according to the sequences correctly guessed, the lowest odds being a single number and the highest on a correct sequence of all five. Put in a nutshell the case for Camelot was that the activity of the defendants was in truth a lottery, but "dressed up" to give it the appearance of betting or wagering, and that the similarities between forty nines and the National Lottery made this apparent. The case for the bookmakers was that in all essential respects forty nines is fixed odds betting and not a lottery, and any similarities with the conduct of the National Lottery were merely of a superficial and marketing character.

Sufficient to say that I found in favour of the defendants and ordered Camelot to pay £600,000 costs. But I have never engaged in the delights of either the National Lottery or forty nines, and as my previous comments will indicate, have no intention whatever of so doing.

... And Tears

If laughter keeps us happy sorrow keeps us human and humanity is a crucial quality on the bench. In ancient Greece two schools of philosophy flourished: the Stoics and Epicureans. The Stoics taught the suppression of human emotions as an antidote to the traumas and troubles of life. The Epicureans advocated the escapist course of concentrating on the pleasures of life. The flaw in both of these philosophies is that they are dehumanising. The cure is worse than the complaint. The two masks in the auditorium represent the complete picture of life. Sadness is an essential part of the human experience and it cannot and should not be evaded. The administration of justice involves a sense of compassion, but this must never lapse into sentimentality. How to apply the one while avoiding the other is never easy. I have met people who seem to think that the work of a stipendiary magistrate consists in the main of dealing with comic characters: cheerful drunks, care-free tramps and saucy prostitutes. These people are neither cheerful nor care-free. They are tragic. They have fallen into a way of life in which the road is downhill all the way. I have always felt a sense of frustration that I can do nothing more useful with such petty offenders than the futile exercise of imposing fines.

Many of those who appear as defendants in magistrates' courts, in contrast to the Crown Courts, are not inherently wicked people at all. They are individuals who simply do not possess the inner resources to cope with the traumas and difficulties of life. They have cracked under pressure. Again-and-again I have read in pre-sentence reports how the descent into crime began with bereavement, divorce, loss of employment or a breakdown in health, physical or mental. The sense of loss or rejection which these things involve can be hard for a well-balanced person to handle, but for less robust personalities they can prove devastating. The crucial adjustments which such situations call for are beyond their capacity to achieve.

I am calling to mind, in this context, the "stalker" type of crime. This frequently, although not always, results from a ruptured relationship, such as a divorce or desertion. I recall one very bad case of threatening phone calls made by the defendant to his ex-wife who was now living with another man. The calls were of a very violent character, threatening dire consequences, even death. I certainly had imprisonment in mind, but the remorse shown by the defendant was something quite out of the ordinary. The calls had been taped and the defendant had experienced horror at the sound of his own voice issuing such threats. He wept throughout the hearing and on the basis of such obviously genuine contrition I was able to suspend the inevitable custodial sentence.

In these sort of cases what begins as a sense of humiliation grows into an obsession. This state of mind was brilliantly portrayed in the film *Fatal Attraction,* though in that instance the stalker was a woman, a not unknown but much rarer situation than the other way round. Stalking can cause terrible fear and anguish and Parliament has very correctly legislated to deal with this specific offence.

It has to be said, however, that sincere remorse is rarely seen on the part of defendants. Among the everyday run of pickpockets, purse snatchers, shoplifters and violent offenders, it is almost unknown. Their main emotion seems to be disappointment at being caught.

Something which I have learnt during a lifetime in the criminal courts, first as counsel and then as judge, is the universality of human weakness. Princes and presidents are compromised by the same impulses that spell trouble for ordinary people. As I write, the President of the United States of America is on trial for perjury and obstruction of justice. Members of the European Commission have been accused of fraudulent conduct. I have seen people with little to gain and everything to lose by indulging in crime, sent to prison thereby bringing disaster upon themselves and their families. At the other end of the scale is the drink-driver whose career has been ruined by disqualification. Pale-faced and shaken, he leaves the dock wondering why on earth he drove his car after the business lunch which might well have enhanced a future now in ruins.

Another cause of much suffering is domestic violence. It presents great problems for the criminal law. On the one hand the higher courts have laid down the principle that it must be treated with the same severity as any other violent conduct. Yet it presents very special dilemmas for both the police and the courts. The police have a natural reluctance to become involved in marital incidents, particularly since it is often difficult to separate facts from lies in an atmosphere of highly charged emotions: the problem for the sentencer is how to punish the violent spouse without making the long-term situation worse than before. Cruelty in the home is the cause of terrible distress, but it is something for which the criminal law is a very imperfect instrument.

There are some cases which combine humour and tragedy. A vagrant offender appeared before me charged with criminal damage. He had 20 previous convictions for precisely the same action — breaking windows. The police officer explained that this was the only means by which he could get a bath, a meal and a roof over his head for a few nights. The defendant waited for an officer to appear and then — bang went the window. He thanked me for the seven days I gave him. Bizarre, almost comic conduct, but also very sad.

CHAPTER 3

Coping with Crime

The first day on which I sat on the bench at Bow Street I received a warm welcome. A lady charged with being drunk in the street demonstrated her respect for the magistrate by removing her shoe and throwing it at me. Happily, as so often happens on such occasions, the aim was faulty and the shoe struck the court clerk who was less than amused. I cannot recall now why I had incurred her wrath, but it made me realise that whatever my job was about popularity was not one of them. When I was sworn in as a stipendiary magistrate by the then Lord Chief Justice, Lord Widgery, I took an oath to do right to all manner of persons without fear or favour, affection or ill-will. I have always taken this to mean that the penalty must fit the offence, regardless of the background, social status or ethnic grouping of the defendant. There must be no favouritism and no prejudice.

It was once my dismal task to sentence a judge to a term of imprisonment. The tale was tragic enough. A County Court judge, who resigned before the case, had pleaded guilty to his third drink-driving offence in 12 years. In these circumstances I felt obliged to impose a sentence of 28 days' imprisonment, a fine of £2,000 and a period of ten years' disqualification. This was one of the most difficult decisions of my career. It was the first case in modern times in which a full-time judge had been jailed. Nevertheless, I was criticised by the Campaign Against Drink Driving for excessive leniency.

On another occasion there appeared before me a group of people engaged in a demonstration, the purpose of which I cannot now recall, save that it was a Christian group protesting against armaments. Their refusal to be bound over resulted in a brief period of incarceration for the group — one of whom was a nun. I was informed that I had jailed the first nun to be so sentenced since the Reformation! Once again I had scored a "first."

The purpose of sentencing is to make the penalty fit the offence—but that object is more easily stated than put into practice. A simple example will illustrate this. One of the minor types of offences which come before my court is that of street trading without a licence. I and a colleague of mine were each hearing such a case one day—the defendants both being umbrella salesmen. In both cases it was said to be raining at the time. During the luncheon adjournment we compared notes about the sentence each of us had passed. I said that I had lowered the fine because as it was raining I considered he was performing a public service. "Strange," he replied, "I increased it because by the same token I felt he was making a bigger profit." This simple example illustrates the different considerations which can make sentencing such a difficult exercise.

One rarely ends up being popular with the defendant whatever one does, although leniency is sometimes appreciated. I can only recall one instance when this applied to severity. A woman appeared before me who pleaded guilty to shoplifting. I use the term "woman" because I am not of that generation which employs the ubiquitous terms "lady" or "gentleman" in a manner which deprives these words of their dictionary meaning. She had four previous convictions for the same type of offence for which she had twice been conditionally discharged and twice fined. This time I felt enough was enough and sent her to prison for 30 days. Some considerable time later I was walking to court one morning when the same woman approached me in a spirit of great good will with a smiling face. "Do you remember me, Mr Bartle?" she said. Somewhat taken aback I replied, truthfully, that I did not. "You sent me to prison for my fifth offence of shoplifting, I have never done it again and never will."

On the subject of sentencing generally, it is an extremely important topic and one which is not merely the concern of judges, lawyers and criminologists. Every citizen has an interest and a degree of involvement.

I have no doubt that I may be accused of adopting a simplistic approach in what I have to say. My answer is that although I have not made a study of the subject in the academic sense, I have sat on the bench for 26 years which has given me, I believe, greater practical insights than many of those who write and expound on the subject, but who have never exposed themselves to the position of facing the practical side of this topic.

The subject of sentencing and the purpose it seeks to achieve is vast, and countless books have been devoted to it. Some, like those of Professor D A Thomas,[1] are of great value to the practitioner. Others are much less so. Their authors are intelligent, sometimes learned, people who have devoted much time to the study of the subject. It is also true to say that many of those who pronounce and dogmatise on this topic have had little or no experience of actually sitting in judgment and facing the responsibility of passing sentence, with very little time for consultation with others or even with oneself, upon those who, day after day, year after year appear in magistrates' and Crown Courts up and down the country. I do not mean by this that the absence of practical experience in itself undermines the value of anyone's views. What must be borne in mind, however, is that the theorist and the practitioner think in very different ways. The theorist concerns himself or herself with the underlying purpose of sentencing. Is that purpose to deter, to reform or to enforce retribution? The practitioner knows that different considerations apply in each individual case. Professor Thomas, in his classic work on the subject *Principles of Sentencing* puts it this way: "The sentencer is presented with a choice: he may impose, usually in the name of general deterrence, a sentence intended to reflect the offender's culpability, or he may seek to influence his future behaviour by subjecting him to an appropriate measure of supervision, treatment or preventative confinement."

Now let me introduce some views, others might say prejudices, of my own, garnered over many years on the bench. The philosophy of sentencing has become an academic subject. Universities have departments devoted to criminology and the response of society to crime.

---

1. I have not ordinarily included "obituaries" in this book although a number of those I mention have died. But David Thomas (1938–2013) had such an enormous influence in developing the law and practice of sentencing in Britain that I believe I should in his case. He was the commanding authority on the subject ever since the publication of his magnificent *Principles of Sentencing* (1970), when he was 31. The book was "a landmark of legal scholarship, a great achievement based on an analysis of the work of the Court of Appeal on sentencing between 1962 and 1969. In this study, he distilled the principles that were to influence the conduct of the courts in a crucially important area of law that hitherto had been largely neglected": for further details, see https://www.theguardian.com/law/2013/nov/05/david-thomas

Libraries are replete with tomes on the subject. Judges and magistrates are subjected to directives and guidelines. Training exercises and seminars are held and the Magistrates' Association publishes sentencing guidelines for the benefit of its members. All of this is in pursuit of more competent, consistent and less diverse sentencing, and to criticise these efforts would be negative and unhelpful. But I do believe such endeavours have their limits, which should be recognised. I say that for the following reasons. First, I believe sentencing to be an art, not a science. General principles there may be, but only the broadest guidance is of value to the bench in the myriad of circumstances and situations which have to be grappled with in the course of the day's work. This is especially true for stipendiary magistrates. Secondly, the principle of judicial independence overrides all attempts at anything approximating to uniformity of approach. Thirdly, the whole concept of conformity in this area is, frankly, moonshine. I recall as a young member of the Bar appearing in cases at the Central Criminal Court. We advocates knew for a certainty that some judges were lenient in sentencing while others were severe. We hoped to have our cases listed in the courts of the "softer" tribunals.

The basic principles of sentencing can, I believe, be quite simply stated. First, consider the degree of gravity of the offence; secondly study the character and background history of the defendant; thirdly take into account any mitigating circumstances attaching to either. The three purposes of sentencing are punishment, deterrence and reformation. I do not believe that sentencing by the courts produces any deterrence at all in the general sense. I do not think that anyone says to themselves "I must not commit this crime because I read in the newspapers that someone received a heavy sentence for doing the same thing." An individual may be deterred by a particular form of sentence in his or her own case such as a suspended term of imprisonment, but personally I fear that most community sentences do not normally have this effect. They do not have a sufficiently severe sanction for their breach. In my view community sentences would be more effective if accompanied by a suspended prison sentence which would take effect immediately on breach of the former.

In recent years there has been much legislation on the subject of sentencing. Some has been constructive and helpful, some anything but. The Criminal Justice Act 1991 was an example of the latter. Two features of the Act gave rise to the utmost concern on the part of adjudicators. The first was the provision which required courts virtually to disregard previous convictions for the purpose of sentencing. The second introduced the system of unit fines. The latter, in particular, drove a number of justices of the peace to resign in despair of legislation which was producing utterly ludicrous results.

I deal first with the unit fines. This was a classic instance of the folly of over-formalisation. The spirit behind it appears to have been expressed by the Permanent Under-Secretary to the Home Office at the time, David Faulkner, who was quoted in *The Times* (April 4, 1993) as saying "Under the previous system there was widespread confusion, with courts sentencing on a cafeteria principle—choosing whichever sentence suited their task at the time—instead of working in a controlled and consistent framework." It has always seemed strange to me that judges and magistrates should be appointed to the bench and yet not be trusted to exercise their judicial sense properly. Sentencing is not a matter of suiting one's taste. It is a question of fitting correctly the penalty to the offender and the offence, and that is what I and my colleagues, stipendiary and lay, always endeavour to do. The unit fine system was a bureaucratic piece of nonsense in which a formula was created by which all courts everywhere in the country should regulate the size of fines imposed on offenders. Each offence was apportioned a number of "gravity units." The defendant was required to complete a form regarding his or her income, but not capital assets. Expenses were deducted from income and the remaining sum divided by three to arrive at a disposable weekly income. The formula was completed by multiplying the disposable weekly income by the number of appropriate gravity units to compute the fine. One only has to state the proposition to appreciate the problems. First, defendants had to be trusted to complete the forms honestly. Since a number of these were persons of proven dishonest character no such assumptions could be made. Secondly, the test was based on income only, and persons with capital assets, but who also happened to be unemployed at the time, were in a far better position than those who had no assets but a very modest income. Those in work were penalised compared with those who were not. Thirdly, the reduction in gravity of particular offences to comply with a unit measurement was a highly dubious exercise. The consequence of this scheme was not greater conformity in sentencing, but inconsistencies so great that they offended against even a basic sense of justice.

The Government White Paper which preceded the Act was presented to Parliament in February 1990. Among other things it stated:

> "One of the advantages of the unit fine system is in focusing on the disposable income of the offender. The majority of offenders do not have substantial means. A fine which deprives an offender of a substantial part of his disposable weekly income for number of weeks is a penalty with some impact, even if the level of the individual's disposable income is low."

The White Paper further states: "The Government therefore proposes that the law should expressly provide the courts with the power to *vary* fines according to the offender's means. This would be an essential element of a unit fine system."

What I find bizarre about these words of the White Paper, later given statutory effect in the 1991 Act, is that they seem to assume that courts did not already possess the power to vary the fine according to the means of the offender and also, where appropriate, make an instalment order or an order that the fine be paid under the supervision of the probation service. Had not anyone informed the authors of the White Paper that this was so, and had been for a very long time?

Within a very short time of the passing of the Act it was plain that unit fines were a non-starter. Examples abounded. Of two men convicted of fighting in the street one was fined £600 more than the other. A motorist was fined £500 for a parking offence. For driving without a valid MOT certificate another motorist was ordered to pay £300, and so it went on. I recall dealing with two cases one afternoon In the first a prosperous looking man stood convicted of a deliberate fraud concerning the sale of second-hand but allegedly new motor cycles. He was "unemployed" and the fine had to be £75. The next was a minor offence of careless driving.

The defendant was employed and received a comfortable income. The penalty: £500. Small wonder that Lord Taylor, then Lord Chief Justice, said in a speech to Scottish lawyers that parts of the Act "defy common sense." Further confusion was created by the emphasis laid in the 1991 Act on the principle that an offence is not more serious just because the offender has previous convictions, and that a defendant should be sentenced on the offence before the court and not on his or her criminal record. Here again less than justice was done to sentencers. Of course the primary concern of the court is always the current crime that has been committed. But previous convictions are relevant in several regards. First, they indicate the pattern of offending. They also record the types of sentence passed and whether or not the defendant has been deterred from getting into further trouble. Secondly, a study of earlier convictions will reveal whether there is a breach of an order such as a conditional discharge or suspended sentence.

One of the better ideas embodied in the 1991 Act is the combination order. This combines probation and community service thereby, in a sense, reinforcing the effect of each. Community sentencing is certainly of value in that it provides an alternative to imprisonment, a restraint on liberty and a period of supervision. Its weakness is still that too many offenders regard a community sentence as a soft option. In a number of countries supervisory sentences are accompanied by a suspended sentence of imprisonment. This has the "Sword of Damocles" effect, in that the moment the offender breaks the supervision by committing another crime or breaches the conditions, the prison sentence takes effect immediately and imprisonment is imposed. I believe there is a great deal of sense in giving "teeth" to community sentences in this way. It could, in my view, be applied to advantage in probation orders, community service orders and combination orders. If offenders are to be supervised in the community, the community should be assured of its security and by the same token I believe that courts should not be empowered to impose one form of community sentence more than once in the case of an adult defendant.

The philosophy and practice of sentencing has changed a great deal during my 26 years on the bench, and very much indeed since I was called to the Bar in 1954. In earlier times the options consisted of imprisonment, fines, probation and for very trivial matters, absolute and conditional discharges. The increase in the number of alternative disposals has made sentencing a far more difficult art than it was in those days. One noticeable consequence of the change is that dishonesty, of the kind dealt with in a magistrates' court, is rarely the subject of imprisonment. There was a time when any form of dishonesty by a servant, being a breach of trust, would attract an automatic custodial sentence. That is no longer the case today when community service orders are available.

Sentencing the Violent Offender

In my view the normal penalty for violence which results in injury has to be imprisonment, regardless of the previous good character of the defendant. There is so much violence and aggression these days that those who commit it must expect to be sent to prison. One of the strangest phenomena is what has come to be called "road rage." I personally do not drive. If I am in a hurry I take a cab. I have never understood the universal fascination with driving. One who does not do so is considered to be something of an eccentric. The combination of nervous stress and physical inactivity must be the perfect recipe for heart trouble. I recall a case I had of a senior civil servant, a man of normally excellent character and civilised behaviour, appearing in the dock at Bow Street charged with assaulting a bus driver. He thought the bus had "cut him up." He pursued the bus and when it stopped leapt out of his car and launched a furious assault on the driver. For some people driving seems to bring out their worst and most aggressive instincts. Excessive drinking is behind a great deal of criminally aggressive behaviour today. And not only among those we generally term "yobs." I have known a taxi driver, furious about a jaywalking pedestrian, stop his cab, retrieve a baseball bat from the boot of the cab and strike the offending pedestrian with it. What so many offenders seem to fail to understand is that even a moderate intake of alcohol substantially lowers those natural inhibitions which control the emotions.

A more serious instance of violence occurred when the famous footballer, George Best, was enjoying a drink with his ex-Miss World girlfriend in a St James's public house. A man, clearly under the influence of alcohol, who had been previously asked to leave, struck the soccer star on the head with a beer bottle causing a wound which required eight stitches. I had no hesitation in sending the offender to jail.

The sad thing these days is to see how widely violent behaviour has spread across the whole social spectrum. Young men from the City are as inclined to commit it as football hooligans. Police officers, tube staff, bus conductors, doctors and nurses in casualty departments of hospitals—all are subjected to a growing incidence of assaults by people, some of whom are under the influence of drink or drugs. There was a time when it was common for the magistrates' courts to deal with violent offenders, especially young criminals, as though reformation rather than punishment was the correct way to sentence them. I am convinced that the excessively lenient policy of the 1960s and 1970s was partly responsible for breeding a generation of younger people who had little respect for the law. I well recall in those days, as a beginner at the Bar, appearing in magistrates' courts in country and provincial areas representing young offenders in their teens charged with serious acts of violence: it is appropriate to say that I was sometimes staggered at the lenient sentencing the lay justices of that time meted out to young criminals.

It is fair to say that in those days justices of the peace had very little training compared with today. Consequently they were very susceptible to pleas of mitigation which would have been given short shrift by a professional tribunal. It was so fatally easy for lay magistrates to succumb to the blandishments of social inquiry reports[2] which emphasised the advantages of probation as against detention. These were frequently the composition of a new young breed of probation officers and social workers who were opposed to custodial sentences as a matter of principle. Many a time I appeared in cases in which probation orders and even conditional discharges were imposed for serious assaults on police. Things changed when the Court of Appeal began upholding sentences of custody on young violent offenders regardless of whether they were

---

2. Now known as pre-sentence reports.

students engaged in demonstrations or the lower class of drunken young hooligans attacking a bus conductor or ticket collector.

In the juvenile — now termed youth — courts, the situation was every bit as bad. Here the courts were not entirely to blame since the Children and Young Persons Act of 1963 rendered the magistrates virtually impotent. The alternatives in practice were little more than absurdly low fines, supervision orders and conditional discharges. I recall one case in which a juvenile offender appeared before me for the first time as an adult. His previous record revealed two fines of 50 pence and 15 conditional discharges. I am convinced that this type of sentencing encouraged crime and resulted in the explosion of violent crime in the 1980s and 1990s. The criminal courts administered a form of justice which cost them the respect of the criminal and the confidence of the public.

The jurisdiction of Bow Street Court covers the Soho area and in particular that part known as "China Town," which includes Gerrard Street, Lisle Street and part of Shaftesbury Avenue. It is here that Chinese groups known as Triads operate. The police have had a degree of success against them, but although the majority of the Chinese ethnic minority are decent hardworking people, this type of gangster, who extorts money by threats, and sometimes by acts of violence, seems to be endemic in Chinese society. It is interesting to see how, in a completely different culture, violence can erupt almost at the drop of a hat. Its seems to be a common factor in both Chinese and Japanese society that a slight which would be treated lightly in the western world, can cause tremendous offence in the East. An early British traveller in Japan was riding along when he was passed by a group of Samurai warriors. The Samurai raised their caps in greeting, an act of courtesy which was not returned. In consequence he was pulled down from his horse and very rapidly reduced to something resembling chop suey.

I once heard a case on committal at Bow Street involving several Chinese defendants who were charged variously with murder and grievous bodily harm. The background scenario against which it took place was the happy occasion of a wedding party. Toasts were being proposed as is usual in such circumstances. Then it happened that one such toast was not returned, or rather, was ignored. At once the injured party and his friends made a rush for the kitchen where they armed themselves with knives. There followed mayhem in which horrific injuries were inflicted, photographs of which it was my unpleasant duty to see. At least one person died while others needed multiple stitches and blood transfusions in order to survive. The oriental may have a passive exterior, but once the facade is broken it is a very different story.

It is a moot point whether violence depicted in the media incites violent behaviour. What is beyond dispute is that for three decades television screens have been the means by which, in films and plays, brutality and violence have been depicted to an extent never known before. Well meaning bodies have been set up to stem the flow of the material, but these have achieved little. With the advent of the internet the task is well nigh impossible.

The Sex Offender

I am dealing here with the type of sexual offender who comes before a London magistrates' court, not those graver offences of rape, paedophilia and the like which must be tried by a higher tribunal. This is another area in which sentencing has certainly changed over the years. There is today, and I am sure rightly, a more understanding attitude towards those who struggle with sexual problems that sometimes lead them into committing criminal offences. The transvestite caught stealing women's underwear, the otherwise respectable man who exposes himself in public to a woman, the elderly man arrested for kerb crawling. These are examples of the pathetic and depressing cases with which magistrates, particularly in the metropolitan area of London, not infrequently have to deal. But there is a very great difference between those who suffer from sexual imbalance and deviation and those who commercially exploit it. The difference has to be reflected in sentencing.

Shortly after my appointment to the bench I had a case of a man charged with theft of several items from a store. He was asking for 142 other offences to be taken into consideration. They consisted of similar thefts of items of women's underwear: stockings, underslips, panties and so on. Police found most of the items hanging on 30 clothes lines in two rooms. This was a case for probation with medical treatment.

Homosexual solicitation is one of the most difficult types of case in my experience, both to try and to sentence. If, as sometimes happens, the accused man is a person of good character and also of some distinction in life, the issue is who to believe. On the one hand are two police officers who give clear evidence of what they have seen the defendant doing in a public lavatory in order to attract like-minded individuals to commit a sexual act. Yet it may be that the defendant is of excellent character who calls highly presentable character witnesses to vouch for him. As a stipendiary, sitting alone, this has always been for me the type of case to dread. In the absence of any reasonable doubt one has to convict. Yet the consequences for the defendant can be dire.

Are tourists more likely to misbehave in a foreign country because the fact of being far from home reduces their sense of responsibility? I am not sure. Certainly a great many visitors to London from overseas commit shoplifting offences. There is a form of indecent assault which I might be tempted to call the "Buckingham Palace assault," since so many of the cases I get occur at the Changing of the Guard, or some such traditional ceremony. It consists of the male culprit (this type of misdemeanour is a masculine affair) thrusting his pelvic region into the hind quarters of the woman in front. The satisfaction gained from such activity must be remarkably limited. One of the problems of trying this kind of case is the invariable absence of the woman in question. The prosecution case consists only of police observation, and this, in a crowd, is not always of the most convincing quality. Similar offences occur on crowded tube trains, an atmosphere which perhaps, for some, creates a degree of temptation.

This sort of infringement of the law are fairly minor matters, although they can cause distress, and are generally dealt with by a fine and bind-over to be of good behaviour. But sexual obsession can create a far more serious, and sometimes potentially dangerous situation. For some curious reason it sometimes happens that a man cannot understand why his attentions have been rejected. I have experienced instances of this when the defendant has been old enough to be the father of the woman in question. The result is endless telephone calls, letters, following down the street and so on. The danger comes when the rejection causes anger and there are threats of violence, and sometimes violence itself. Such conduct can cause great fear and distress, and, if after a warning, the conduct is resumed, imprisonment may be the appropriate sentence. One tries to avoid this because it may further exacerbate the injured feelings of the defendant.

The most serious cases of sexual crime are those which are committed to the Crown Court. These sometimes involve the terrible perversion of child abuse. I recall as counsel being instructed in a case for one of a group of men some of whom held responsible positions, charged with offences against children. They established premises to which the children were lured to perform sexual acts with them. It was a truly terrible case and the inevitable heavy sentences were passed.

One the saddest cases I heard at Bow Street concerned a man of 78 years-of-age charged with 11 offences of indecent assault upon his own grandchildren. The earliest of the allegations related to an incident 20 years before. The charges ranged from 1974 to 1984, but it was 1991 before matters were reported by the members of the family who had been the victims. The defendant was of previous good character, but the statements of the witnesses certainly constituted a *prima facie* case. I was requested by the defence to dismiss the case on the grounds of abuse of process. This doctrine has been much invoked in recent years. It applies when the lapse of time between the alleged crime and trial is such, or the process of the court has been so wrongly manipulated, that the defendant is deprived of the possibility of a fair trial. This issue, which these days arises quite frequently, can be very difficult to decide. It was pleaded that because of his age and poor state of health the defendant would be unable, after such a lapse of time, to recall his whereabouts and to provide himself with an alibi, probe inconsistencies in the prosecution case, give proper instructions to those acting for him or stand the stress of the proceedings without endangering his life.

The rule with most decisions by a magistrate is that reasons do not have to be given, but in more serious matters, for example extradition and decisions of significant points of law, it is recognised that reasons, though not a full judgment, should be given.³ It was clear that the defendant was not in a position to say "there were witnesses who could have established my innocence but they have died," or "I don't know their whereabouts" or "they are no longer willing to give evidence." If that had been the case his prospects of a fair trial would indeed have been gravely prejudiced. But that was not so. The very secretiveness with which crimes of that kind are carried out precludes the availability of witnesses for the defence and the defendant is thrown back on his own uncorroborated denials. Moreover, here was a case, as stated by the Crown's witnesses, where a man had concealed his crimes, exploited a grandpaternal relationship and rewarded the victims with sweets warning them to keep quiet. Hence the delay. Finally, alibi was not an issue in the case. The offences could not have been committed by someone else. Either the defendant was guilty or he was not. I had no difficulty in finding that the public interest required that I dismiss the application, and send the defendant for trial.

Prosecutions under the Obscene Publications Act are common at Bow Street. So also are those in respect of "peep shows" and unlicensed sex shops. Those who complain that legislation against pornography and the censorship of films and television programmes is an infringement of "freedom" do not understand the distinction between liberty and licence. The great majority of people manifestly do not want the nation flooded with pornographic films, magazines and television programmes. Those who do, and others who exploit them for gain, are in the position of a minority attempting to enforce its prurient tastes on an unwilling majority. To permit this would be a violation of three important principles: public morality, the rule of law and the democratic ideal.

Sentencing the Minor Drug Offender

Concerning the terrible menace to our society of drug addiction, here I deal only with the minor offender whom I have to sentence at Bow Street Court from time-to-time. Sentencing offenders at this end of the scale of seriousness is not easy merely because the offences are of a minor

---

3. There is since 2003 a more general and statutory duty to give reasons for sentencing decisions.

nature. The guidelines on sentencing those convicted of crimes in connection with the possession and supply of prohibited drugs have been laid down by the Lord Chief Justice, but those directions concern the appropriate length of imprisonment for major offenders. They do not apply to the type of offence with which magistrates' courts are familiar, which consist in the main of the possession of small quantities of cannabis, crack cocaine or ecstasy. When the charge is one of supplying or possession with intent to supply, it frequently consists of one confirmed addict providing another with a portion of his own narcotic, sometimes obtained on prescription. In some ways sentencing a minor offender can be more difficult. The issue, unlike that of graver cases, is not simply how long should the term of imprisonment be. For the minor drug criminal a greater range of options is available to the court. Finding the right one can be a problem.

Let me first of all take offences of possession only. I cannot recall ever sending anyone to prison for possession of a small quantity of class B, or for that matter class A, drugs. The amount would have to be very substantial before I personally would consider custody. These are people with a severe problem who need help. If there is a pattern of drug misuse in the past history of the defendant, medical and pre-sentence reports on the up-to-date position should generally be obtained. This is because addiction to drugs can lead to drug-fuelled crime, and this is a trend which should, if possible, be interrupted. The danger for the sentencer is that drug-motivated offences may appear on the record to be merely a history of dishonesty. Nevertheless, I do believe that crime, in all its forms, is largely a matter of choice. There was a time when much mitigation was along the lines that a defendant had a craving for alcohol and committed the crime under the influence of drink. Now advocates plead drug addiction. But drugs, like drink, are taken voluntarily, in many cases by people who think that what they are doing should not in any event infringe the law. For a first offence of possession a conditional discharge may be appropriate; for a second a fine, and for a third a community sentence such as probation or a community service order. But continuing contempt for the law in this or any other sphere must eventually attract a prison sentence.

Quite different considerations apply to crimes of supplying and possession with intent to supply. In these cases, even when the amounts involved are small, the defendant is involving others and this is a serious factor even when the supplying is not on a commercial basis. Where there is a commercial element the powers of sentencing of a magistrates' court are generally inadequate and the defendant should be sent to the Crown Court. But supply offences involving class A drugs must normally be met by a custodial sentence from three to six months. It is crucially important, in the opinion of the author, that the message does not go out that the magistrates' courts are "soft" on drugs.

There are voices today clamouring for a radical change in the law regarding drug misuse. They are calling for the legalisation, or as they prefer to put it, the decriminalisation of the possession and supply of class B, and some go so far as to say class A, drugs. Frankly I can see little or no difference between legalisation and decriminalisation. The effect is precisely the same. These appeals should, I believe, be firmly resisted both now and in the future: they are a counsel of despair.

One has to approach the problem of drug addiction and of drug-related crime in a spirit of realism. As with all other forms of crime, containment is the most that can be achieved. Neither government nor all the welfare bodies and agencies working in conjunction can save individuals from the consequences of their own conduct unless they are willing to co-operate in their own rescue. To say that decriminalisation would remove offenders from the judicial process may well be literally true, but the same could be said of shoplifters. Only one tenth of an iceberg is above water level, but a ship which for that reason ignored icebergs would share the fate of the *Titanic*.

Let me set out my own arguments against decriminalisation. First, this would be a policy which completely fails to address the problem of drug-related crime. Like alcoholism, drug addiction is behind a great deal of "street" crime; assaults, street robbery, criminal damage, theft and so on. In a free for all, even were this confined to cannabis, youngsters would acquire the "Dutch courage" from smoking cannabis needed to break the law. Secondly, it would create a "pushers' paradise." Small suppliers are themselves supplied by major dealers. The inflow of cannabis into the country would become a flood. Just as thieves depend on receivers, so suppliers depend upon a ready market. With all restraints removed this would become a cascade. Thirdly, what sort of message would such a policy send out to young people who have been advised by teachers and parents to resist the blandishments of friends to join them in a "joint"? At every "rave up" the hash would be as available as the drinks. Fourthly, there is the lesson from other countries. The most liberal drug laws in Europe are those of Holland—yet the problems to which this attitude has given rise are causing the Dutch authorities to think again. At the International Summit on Drug Misuse in 1990 which I was privileged to attend, every one of the 300 or so governments represented opposed the legalisation of cannabis.

The argument derived from a comparison of alcohol and cannabis has no substance: there is the obvious point that two wrongs do not constitute a right. Alcohol abuse is just as socially destructive as drug misuse. There is, however, the difference that there is ample evidence to show that addicts frequently graduate from soft to hard drugs. There is generally no such progression with alcohol, at least not among young people and not to such an extent.

Finally, there is the new dimension to the situation created by Aids. It is well known, hypodermic needles, infected with the Aids virus, have been a potent factor in the spreading of Aids among young, intravenous addicts. Nowhere has this been seen more tragically than in Edinburgh where the incidence of Aids among young people is particularly high. But in addition to this consideration there is the likelihood of narcotics, including cannabis, inducing an attitude that conduces to casual sexual behaviour and that in its turn increases the possibility of contracting Aids.

My experience in the realm of drug misuse has not been confined to my work on the bench: I have attended several major international conferences on this subject and have also been privileged to serve on the Home Office Advisory Council on the Misuse of Drugs for a number of years.

In November 1989 I was invited to act as vice-chairman at a conference of West African states which had been convened to discuss the drug-trafficking situation in West Africa. The conference was held in Lome, in Togo, which is a former French colony. The states represented were

Togo, Benin, Burkina-Faso, Cameroon, Ivory Coast, Gambia, Guinea, Mali, Nigeria, Senegal and Sierra Leone. It was my first visit to West Africa. I had never before experienced such heat, but nor had I previously seen the poverty of a small third world African state. Yet the people had a strange natural dignity of manner and their attire was colourful. The delegates represented a broad cross-section of people connected with law enforcement and drug misuse in the region: magistrates, police officers, a minister of justice, doctors and chemists and so on. The conference was lively and interesting and the exchange of views was of great interest. I was impressed with the way in which small third world states with very limited resources were confronting seemingly mountainous problems. There was something intensely moving about that. Cannabis was endemic in these countries and together with other psychotropic plants had been part of the life of village communities for generations. The chances of doing anything about this were precisely nil. Heroin and cocaine had made their appearance more recently and had achieved rapid popularity with younger people, largely among the better off families. These were derived from transit across Africa and came from the Golden Crescent (Pakistan, Afghanistan and Iran) the Golden Triangle (South-East Asia and Thailand) and from South America. The narcotics came via airports such as Lagos, Abidjan and Dakar and some by overland route via Turkey for onward journey to Europe. It is only within recent years that a serious problem relating to class A drugs has developed in the region.

We learnt that the problem in West Africa is not the production of heroin and cocaine, as in South America, but one of transit. The general state of poor health in the area makes the situation much worse. Vitamin deficiency in the body increases the adverse effects of drugs. Further aggravating factors are the influx of people from the country into the cities, the spread of Aids, the general ignorance about personal hygiene, the shortage of proper medical facilities and the terrible conditions in the prisons. The poor state of the economies of most of the countries in the region ruled out high technological responses to the problem.

I was able, on my return home, to make recommendations to the appropriate government agencies regarding assistance to some of the countries for the building of laboratories, hospital accommodation, the training of security officers, improved prison conditions, treatment centres and education of the young. My only unpleasant recollections of the conference were periodic bouts of African tummy: having received all the proper injections and taken the right pills, I still found that the best antidote was to sit in a hot bath and consume liberal doses of whisky!

On April 9 to 11, 1990 I attended the World Ministerial Drugs Summit held at the Queen Elizabeth II Conference Centre in London which was attended by presidents and ministers from nations throughout the world. The stated objectives of the conference were to maintain the momentum of international co-operation on drugs developed at previous international conferences; to increase international commitment to reducing the demand for drugs; to develop the effectiveness of demand reduction policies through the exchange of expertise and to identify effective methods to combat demand, production and trafficking of cocaine. It goes without saying that these were indeed ambitious targets. Among those present was President Barco of Columbia whom it was my pleasure and privilege to meet on a subsequent occasion.

The conference was opened by the Prime Minister, Margaret Thatcher. Mrs Thatcher with the clarity so characteristic of her style, set out the role of the conference and the extent of the drug menace facing the world today. The particular aspect of the conference, she stated, was demand reduction. In this connection she set out six areas in which immediate and urgent action was necessary: first, the education of young people in the terrible consequences of drug abuse and the threat it constitutes to their health and future; secondly, a greater effort in advertising and publicity; thirdly, a programme to strengthen the importance of the family and the community; fourthly, the identification of addicts at an early stage; fifthly, a greater effort into treatment and rehabilitation, and sixthly, and (here I quote)

> "We should make it absolutely clear that you can't beat drug-taking by legalising drugs. That is the way to destroy young lives, ruin families and undermine society itself. Our task is to protect young people, not deliberately expose them to danger. I can assure you that our government will never legalise illicit drugs, hard or soft."

That was a view endorsed by the entire conference, and, happily, followed by every government in Britain since Mrs Thatcher's.

Notwithstanding the principles emphasised at the conference and many excellent efforts made and initiatives undertaken by the various agencies involved in this country, the situation remains very serious—so serious that the only practical policy is one of containment and harm reduction. A Department of Health statistical bulletin published in March 1998 revealed that during the six months' period ending September 30, 1996 in England the number of individual users presenting to agencies (24,879) showed a rise of seven per cent from the previous six months' period; over half of these users presenting were in their 20s and one in eight were aged under 20; heroin is still the main drug of misuse accounting for 58 per cent of users, an increase from 54 per cent in the previous period while 45 per cent of users, whose injecting status in the last four weeks was known, reported having injected in the last four weeks.

The new government's strategy has four elements: first, to help and educate young people in the dangers of drug misuse in order to enable them to achieve their full potential in society; secondly, to protect our communities from drug-related anti-social and criminal behaviour; thirdly, to enable people with drug problems to overcome them and live healthy and crime-free lives, and fourthly, to stifle the availability of illegal drugs on our streets. The success of these aims is vital to the well-being of our nation.

CHAPTER 4

Policemen Under Fire

The Wapping Riots

During the 21 years I have been at Bow Street there have been a number of occasions on which the defendants in the dock have been police officers. The law is quite clear: police officers, both as witnesses and as accused persons, are to be treated in the same way as all other citizens They do not enjoy a privileged position, but nor, on the other hand, should they suffer prejudice because of their profession. There is, I believe, a very great danger of presuming guilt on the part of an accused officer. The reasoning tends to be: policemen are there to protect the public from crime and to enforce the law. Therefore, if a policeman is charged with a criminal offence, that is an indication that he or she is one of the "black sheep" of the service. Nothing could be more unfair. The police undoubtedly do include among their number corrupt and brutal officers who accept bribes and commit acts of violence. When they are caught they receive severe punishment. But policemen, like others, are sometimes wrongly accused by those who have their own reasons for hating law enforcers, and who grasp at any opportunity to blacken their characters. I well remember, when I was at the Bar, the numberless cases in which we, as defence counsel, were instructed by our clients to accuse police officers of "planting" incriminating materials such as drugs, offensive weapons or stolen property onto the defendant. In a few instances this accusation may have had substance. In a great many the suggestion was without foundation. Corruption and violence there will always be from a small minority in the police. It is frequently detected and invariably met with condign punishment.

Two cases of outstanding interest involving allegations of crime against the police came before me at Bow Street. They both resulted in the officers concerned being cleared, but led to myself being wholly unjustifiably accused in certain quarters of being biased in favour of the police.

The first of these involved a very serious disturbance, amounting virtually to a riot in Wapping in the East End of London on Saturday, January 24, 1987. This date marked the anniversary of Mr Rupert Murdoch's transfer of four national newspapers to Wapping and the consequent sacking of 5,000 staff. Needless to say this was a policy which greatly inflamed the feelings of the printing workers, but nothing had prepared the authorities for the violence of the events which took place that night. Between 12,000 and 15,000 people were directly involved and the almost unprecedented number of 12,000 police attended the scene. As an indication of what the police had to cope with, it was reported that more than 200 pieces of concrete and broken paving stones were hurled at police lines. A severed pig's head was impaled on the railings outside the News International plant near the police cordon, and at the end of the night more than three tons of missiles — including cast iron railings, scaffolding poles, fence posts, ball-bearings and bottles, were collected. One-hundred-and-ninety policemen were injured, as were 99 other people.

Following that night of violence and mayhem more than 500 complaints were made by 185 people who were at Wapping. Some officers were disciplined. Twenty-six were charged with criminal offences which included assault, conspiracy to pervert or obstruct justice, and perjury. This was the largest number of police officers to be charged with offences arising out of a single incident.

The inquiry into police conduct at Wapping was carried out by Northamptonshire Police and included an analysis of 23 hours of video recordings, 695 photographs and 3,024 documents. One of the 26 police who were charged was absent abroad. The remaining 25 appeared before the court in groups. The six who appeared before myself faced charges that between January 27, 1987 and February 3, 1988 they conspired together to pervert the course of justice by making false entries in their report books. This related to the arrest of three men at a public house during the demonstrations. When I heard the case, charges were pending against 19 other officers. Their fate depended to a large extent on the outcome of the trial involving the six.

It will be noted that there was a substantial time-lag between the date of the alleged crimes and the date of the hearing. Later on, after I had dismissed the case, newspapers referred to the defendants as having been "acquitted." This was not in fact the position and the true situation requires some explanation for those who are not lawyers.

It is of the essence of a criminal trial that the accused person has a fair hearing and that nothing should occur, so far as can be avoided, to interfere with that right. If the defendant has been so prejudiced because of undue and unreasonable delay or because there has been improper manipulation of the court process, the court of trial, which includes a court of committal, has a discretion to rule that an abuse of process has occurred and therefore the prosecution should be stayed and the defendant discharged. Moreover, in certain circumstances mere delay which gives rise to prejudice and unfairness may in itself amount to an abuse of process. The key question is: has the accused person been deprived of the opportunity to receive a fair trial?

The prejudice resulting from delay is obvious. Memory fades, witnesses die or disappear and documents are lost. In the particular case which I was trying the defence emphasised that investigators knew of the allegations against the six by June 1987, but the officers were not warned or put on notice about the complaints until December 1987. They were not interviewed until February 1988 and were not arrested and charged until January 1989. A total of 11 policemen were interviewed and 42 files were sent to the Director of Public Prosecutions. The defence submitted further that the Crown Prosecution Service decision not to proceed against any one officer until a decision had been made against all of them was wrong, and that in justice individuals must be informed at the outset that complaints have been made against them. Previous cases were cited involving police officers which supported this contention.

In staying the proceedings for abuse of process I commented: "There can be no doubt at all that there has been a substantial delay in investigations of these alleged offences. There has also been a considerable delay in notifying the officers of the allegations." I concluded that nobody could be expected to recall events that happened over a year ago.

The Director of Public Prosecutions decided to challenge my ruling in the Queen's Bench Divisional Court. The case came before Lord Justice Watkins and Mr Justice Garland on December 19, 1989. The principles established by the court were threefold. First, in criminal proceedings mere delay which gives rise to prejudice and unfairness may itself amount to an abuse of process Secondly, in some circumstances prejudice would be presumed from substantial delay. In the absence of a presumption, where there was substantial delay it would be for the prosecution to justify it. Thirdly, in cases involving police officers the circumstances of service of a notice under regulation 7 of the Police (Discipline) Regulations (SI 1985 No. 581) were a material consideration which the court was entitled to take into account. The court also heard the appeal of another officer in respect of whom the question of abuse of process had been decided differently by Mr Wicks, a colleague of mine.

Regulation 7 of the 1985 Regulations states:

> "The investigating officer shall, as soon as is practicable (without prejudicing his or any other investigation of the matter) in writing inform the member subject to investigation of the report, allegation or complaint and give him a written analysis: (a) informing him that he is not obliged to say anything concerning the matter, but that he may, if he so desires, make a written or oral statement concerning the matter to the investigating officer or to the chief officer concerned, and (b) warning him that if he makes such a statement it may be used in any subsequent disciplinary proceedings."

In their Lordships' judgment there was extreme delay from which prejudice could properly be inferred. The mere fact that more than a thousand police officers were under investigation in no sense diminished the prejudice suffered by a particular officer against whom there was a *prima facie* case of the commission of a criminal offence at a very early stage of that investigation.

The Director of Public Prosecutions was denied leave to appeal to the House of Lords and the prosecution was discontinued against the remaining defendants.

The Guildford Four Police Officers

This case is one which I shall discuss in a little detail. It was by far the most serious and significant matter in terms of public policy and public concern to come before me during my entire career on the bench. The events involving the bombing of two public houses in Guildford and one in Woolwich in 1974 are still within the memory of many people, most of all those who suffered bereavement in consequence. The term "The Guildford Four" was applied to the four suspects, three young men and a young woman who were subsequently arrested, charged with and convicted of the crimes, and in due course sentenced to substantial terms of imprisonment. The aftermath was the release of the four after their convictions had been quashed, and then there followed the investigation into and prosecution of three police officers against whom it was alleged that they had conspired to falsify note-books and records of interviews with the defendants and so obtained "confessions" which had never in fact been made. Since my role in these events related solely to the charges against the police officers I shall deal only briefly with the background history of the case before coming to the difficult, indeed traumatic task with which I was confronted, and the consequences in terms of adverse publicity which fell to my lot.

At the time of the bombings the three officers were serving in the Surrey Constabulary. Thomas Lionel Style was a Detective Chief Inspector; John Sutherland Donaldson was a Detective Sergeant; Vernon Attwell was a Detective Constable. On October 5, 1974, a bomb exploded at the Horse and Groom public house in Guildford in consequence of which five people were killed and a number of others were seriously injured. Later the same day another bomb exploded at the Seven Stars public house in the city. A month later, on November 7, a further explosion occurred at the King's Arms in Woolwich. The consequence was more death and injury. Needless to say, this wanton carnage aroused public feelings to an unprecedented extent and there was heavy pressure on the police to find the culprits. Among those taken into custody and questioned were the four defendants—Armstrong, Richardson, Hill and Conlon. All four were, in due course, charged and convicted in October 1975 on counts of conspiracy and murder. The prosecution case against the four consisted of confessions which they allegedly made to the police in the course of their inquiries. These were contained in both written statements and statements said by the police to have been given orally during the interviews.

It is no part of this work to discuss the strengths or weaknesses of the evidence in the case of the Guildford Four. These were not in any event matters for my consideration at the hearing at Bow Street, although some newspapers seemed unable or unwilling to understand or accept that fact. They are only relevant in the context of the subsequent charges against the police, and those charges devolved upon one the defendants, Patrick Armstrong.

At the trial of the Four in October 1975 the officers gave evidence that they had interviewed Armstrong on December 4, 5 and 6, 1974 and that a contemporaneous handwritten record had been made of each of these interviews. In addition to this Armstrong made two written statements. In his defence Armstrong maintained that fear of police brutality had caused him to sign the statements, that he had never made the incriminating confessions nor had he taken any part in the bombings. He denied that there had been any interview on December 5, 1974. Armstrong was sentenced to life imprisonment with a recommendation that he serve 35 years' minimum.

The Four applied for leave to appeal against their convictions but this was refused on October 28, 1977. A number of organizations and individuals expressed continuing concern over the case. They called for a further review of the convictions. These matters remained in abeyance for ten years until the beginning of 1987 when material came to light which related to the cases of Richardson, Hill and Conlon. After a study of this material, on July 31, 1987, the Avon and Somerset Constabulary were requested to conduct an investigation. Officers from Avon and Somerset made a collection of files and papers which it was considered were relevant to the case of the Guildford Four, and a number of police officers, which included the three who were subsequently charged, were interviewed. On January 16, 1989 the Home Secretary referred the case of the Guildford Four to the Court of Appeal.[1]

Detective Superintendent Brock was the officer in charge of the Avon and Somerset inquiry and it was at this stage that he decided to make a careful check of the notes and copy notes of the interviews which had been collected. Detective Inspector Bryant, a woman officer, while preparing bundles of statements for the defence, checked the manuscript notes of the police conversations with Patrick Armstrong against some typed notes of the same interviews. It appeared to D I Bryant that there were discrepancies between the manuscript and the typed notes, a fact which she drew to the attention of her superiors. The conclusion reached by the senior officers involved, having noted that certain additions and deletions had been made to the typed notes, was that the typed notes had been made first and those in the manuscript later. This gave rise to the damaging inference that the manuscript notes were not contemporaneous with the interviews as the investigating officers had claimed at the trial of the Four, but had in fact been composed at a later stage, while the typed notes had been altered to conform with the written ones. The three officers concerned were interrogated about this but were unable to provide an explanation after such a long interval. They maintained, however, that the manuscript notes had been made contemporaneously. On two further occasions the three officers were interviewed again, without cautions or regulation 7 notices putting them on notice of possible prosecution having been served, and they replied in the same terms as before.

I should make the point here that after the acquittal of the three former officers at the Old Bailey there was a certain amount of press comment to the effect that the British legal system had produced an illogical result. On the one hand, it was said, the case against the Guildford Four had been shown to be unfounded while, at the same time, those on whose alleged fabricated evidence they were convicted had been acquitted of guilt. As so often throughout this whole case the comments in the press

---

1. A function now carried out by the Justice Secretary and Criminal Cases Review Commission.

were ill-informed. The issues regarding the Guildford Four and those affecting the former officers were dealt with separately in different courts. The case against the Four was found to be unsafe and unsatisfactory while that against the officers was not proved to the satisfaction of the jury. Therefore there was no incongruity, and both the Four and the former police can properly claim to have been cleared in the eyes of the law.

However, in this particular case the Director of Public Prosecutions decided that the uncertainty about the validity of the notes had rendered the convictions unsafe and on October 19, 1989, when the appeals of the Guildford Four were heard, counsel for the Crown told the court that the Crown would no longer seek to uphold the convictions for the reason that evidence had come to light which showed, in the Crown's view, that the manuscript notes of the interviews on December 4, 5 and 6, were not contemporaneous records. It is important to note the way in which the case was put for the Crown, because the Lord Chief Justice proceeded to make comments which went considerably further than the prosecution position at that stage. Having expressed the view that the officers "must have lied" he went on to say, "In any event the police were not telling the truth about this criminal document in the case against Armstrong. If they were prepared to tell this sort of lie, then the whole of their evidence becomes suspect and, I repeat, on their evidence depended the prosecution case." This contrasts sharply with the penultimate paragraph of the prosecution opening note with which I was provided when the case came before me upon committal at Bow Street: *"The Crown cannot contend that Armstrong did not admit to these crimes* but the inference that can be drawn from the evidence available is that *Armstrong did not provide the information given in the manner reflected by these notes."*

On June 4, 1991 I heard the committal proceedings at Bow Street in which the former police officers stood charged with conspiracy to pervert the course of justice. Well before this date, however, the press had been in full cry. That same press, which had previously lambasted the police for dilatoriness in bringing to book the murderers who had killed and maimed the innocent, now became champions of law and liberty against allegedly corrupt policemen. Typical headlines were "The bent copper" (*Daily Mirror,* October 20, 1989), "The liars—bomb case police fixed the evidence" (*The Sun,* October 20, 1989), "The lies that cost pub 4 their youth" (*Star,* October 20, 1989), "How far did the corruption go?" (*The Independent,* October 20, 1989). These are but a few of the many adverse press notices which the police officers involved received. Yet none had at that time been interviewed as prospective defendants let alone charged with any criminal offence. That point was made eloquently and forcefully by Mr Brian Hayes, Chief Constable of the Surrey Constabulary in a letter to *The Surrey Advertiser* dated October 27, 1989.

The fundamental principle of justice in this country which the press comment quoted above grossly violated is the presumption of innocence. There is a presumption that anyone charged with a criminal offence is innocent until proved to be guilty. This golden rule of our criminal law received scant attention from newspapers which were more interested in sensational reporting than fairness and accuracy.

At the Bow Street hearing, Mr Edmund Lawson, QC, who appeared for the defendants, submitted, as a preliminary issue, that the proceedings should be stayed since their continuance would be an abuse of the process of the court. I have already dealt briefly with the legal doctrine of abuse of process. It gives a court power to stop a prosecution in its tracks when events have occurred which effectively prevent the prospect of a fair and just trial of the accused from taking place. It has nothing to do with the issue of guilt or innocence. I emphasise this because the bitter criticism to which I was subjected in the press displayed a complete ignorance of the grounds on which my decision was based. Mr Lawson submitted on behalf of the defendants that in all the circumstances the delay/elapse of time since the acts complained of had prejudiced them and/or resulted in their being unable to have a fair trial, such prejudice/unfairness having been increased by the adverse publicity. In view of the importance of this case I shall set out my judgment in full:

> "Normally magistrates are not required to give reasons for their decisions, but the Divisional Court of the High Court has commented on more than one occasion that it would be helpful, in cases coming before that court for judicial review if magistrates gave reasons for their decisions, and that those reasons should consist of more than a mere brief statement. Since I

anticipate that my ruling, be it either way, will in due course be reviewed by the Divisional Court, I shall proceed to deliver a judgment which will not be exhaustive, but will I trust, amply cover the grounds on which I reach my conclusion.

First of all I would like to make a preliminary observation which I feel is necessary in view of the great attention which this whole matter has received in the media and among the public at large. My function at this stage is to rule upon an application made on behalf of these three defendants—who I shall henceforth refer to as the applicants—to stay this prosecution on the ground that because of the delay between the events which are the subject of the charges and this pre-committal hearing, taken together with other factors which I shall refer to shortly, these applicants have suffered, and would suffer at their trial, a degree of prejudice from which it can be inferred on the balance of probabilities that a fair trial is no longer possible. That this would amount to an abuse of the process of the court since it is an inherent duty of every court to ensure that justice is done to the defence as well as to the prosecution. That is the issue before me, and such evidence as I have heard relates only to that question. Let me make it abundantly clear that I am not deciding the guilt or innocence of these applicants. I am not even inquiring into whether or not there is a *prima facie* case for them to answer. Therefore my ruling will be no comment whatever on the ultimate issue of guilt or innocence. That would be for a jury, and not for me.

The burden of my task has been greatly eased by the fact that Counsel on both sides are in agreement about the law of abuse of process. That law is not anchored in statute but is a doctrine based on the principle that in criminal trials fairness and justice must be done to both the prosecution and the defence. It is a doctrine which has developed with remarkable rapidity in recent years. I certainly do not intend to go through all the authorities: I have been referred to the relevant case-law and I therefore intend very briefly to say how I understand the law to be on this subject at present and then apply it to the circumstances of this case.

In the leading case of the *Queen and Derby Justices, ex parte Brooks* 1984, the Divisional Court, presided over by the Lord Chief Justice, defined an abuse of process as arising if either:

> the prosecution have manipulated or misused the process of the court so as to deprive the defendant of a protection provided by the law or to take unfair advantage of a technicality, or

> on the balance of probability the defendant has been, or will be, prejudiced in the preparation or conduct of his defence by delay on the part of the prosecution which is unjustifiable; for example not due to the complexity of the inquiry, and preparation of the prosecution case, or to the action of the defendant or his co-accused, or to genuine difficulty in effecting service.

More recent cases referred to were those of *Cherry and Goodger and Others*, more popularly known as the *Wapping Cases*, which came before the Divisional Court in October and December 1989. There, as here, the applications were on behalf of police officers, who were charged with offences alleged to have been committed during the demonstrations at Wapping in January 1987. In those cases the fault for the delay in both the service of regulation 7 notices and the commencement of the proceedings could be laid at the door of the prosecuting authority. The submission of abuse was upheld.

Most heavily relied upon by the defence, however, is the *Queen and Telford Justices, ex parte Badhan* which was heard by the Divisional Court on December 21, 1990 This case extended the law beyond *Brooks* and, it was conceded on both sides, laid down the principles which represent the law as it now stands, and which in my view have considerable significance for the case before me. Those principles are as follows:

> It is not a determinant factor whether any delay or 'elapse of time' is justifiable or justified, contrary to the impression given in *Brooks*. It is not a condition precedent to exercising the abuse of process jurisdiction

in a 'delay' case that the delay is shown to have been caused by some culpable act or omission on the part of the prosecutor or the police.

Where delay is unjustifiable 'and an accused can show on the balance of probability that he has been or will be prejudiced in the preparation or conduct of his defence, then an abuse should be found'.

'An elapse of time for which the prosecuting authorities are not to blame can be such that an accused can be heard to say that a fair trial is no longer possible and the committal proceedings would therefore be an abuse of process'.

Prejudice and/or an inability to have a fair trial may be inferred without proof of specific prejudice.

'…where the elapse of time is a long one, it may be inferred that a fair trial is no longer possible. Whether it is legitimate to draw the inference will depend upon the circumstances of the case.'

This last point is of great importance in this case because the period of 17 years is long by any standards.

I was helpfully directed to a number of other important authorities, but since those I have quoted set out the current position in law I do not propose to refer to any further cases on this subject."

I shall now turn to the facts placed before me, which I shall deal with as concisely as I can.

"In 1974 these three were police officers in the Surrey Constabulary. Mr Style was a Detective Chief Inspector, Mr Donaldson a Detective Sergeant and Mr Attwell a Detective Constable. The case centres upon what occurred during interviews conducted by these three with Patrick Armstrong, one of the Guildford Four, as they have come to be known in the course of police investigations into the bombings of public houses in Guildford and Woolwich in October and November of 1974.

The case for the Crown is that these applicants manufactured and put forward notes of interviews which they falsely asserted were contemporaneous notes of those interviews with Patrick Armstrong. It is said that these notes were not in fact contemporaneously written, but written up later in time. The foundation of the Crown's case rests on the existence of some rough typed notes containing typed and handwritten deletions and amendments which came to be examined in May 1989, having been found in the archives of the Surrey Constabulary by the Avon and Somerset police, who had been entrusted by the Home Secretary in 1987 with the task of conducting an inquiry into certain aspects of the Guildford Four case. The Crown maintain that comparison of the manuscript with the rough typed notes indicate that the typed notes must have been drawn up before the manuscript ones, and therefore the applicants told lies when they claimed in court that the handwritten notes were made at the time of the interviews. There is no suggestion by the Crown that during the 15 years that the suspect notes lay in Surrey police files any attempt was made by anyone to interfere with them. These allegations are emphatically denied by the defence who maintain the notes were properly taken. That is the issue in a nutshell, and I do not want to involve myself in any further discussion of the evidence because, I say yet again, I am not trying the case itself, I am deciding the question of prejudice amounting to abuse, and to that matter I now turn.

One has to start on the basis that the lapse of time in this case has been very great. It is, to the best of my knowledge, much longer than in any of the preceding authorities, except for the case of *Randle and Pottle*, but that case is easily distinguishable from this in that the defendants, having published a book making full admission of the offence charged, could not effectively claim to have been prejudiced. The Crown say that the substantial lapse of time, 17 years, cannot amount to an abuse of process because this case devolves solely upon documentary evidence. I cannot accede to that submission. This is not like a simple case where the question revolves around disputed fingerprints or handwriting. In a trial of these applicants a variety of matters would be argued and debated: what system of interviewing suspects was employed by the Surrey police in 1974? What was the procedure to be followed? What degree of supervision was exercised by senior officers over junior? In what circumstances were typed notes of interviews made and by whom? What was the filing system and how was information relating to one interview transferred to officers questioning other persons? And so on. Justice would certainly not be done by the jury merely examining the two sets of notes and then retiring to consider its verdict. In my view, although this is not a case where it can be said the extreme delay is the fault of the prosecution, I think the lapse of time is such as to give rise to an inference of prejudice. But the defence go further and point to significant examples of the way in which a fair trial would be rendered improbable. First, the detective officers of the Surrey Constabulary were under general orders from the Chief Constable to keep detailed diaries of day-to-day duties. These were routinely destroyed after three years and are no longer available for reference. Secondly, a Detective Sergeant, who might have been able to give important evidence regarding the interviews, died in 1984. Thirdly, and most importantly, every single person who had any dealings, directly or indirectly, with the *Armstrong* case, has no or no proper recollection of the material events. Here I refer to 21 police officers and several typists. Their inability to remember may be ascribed to the passage of time or perhaps to a reluctance to be involved with men who, long before they were charged, let alone convicted, were buried under an avalanche of condemnation. Either way, the effect must be prejudicial to the defence. The prosecution say comparison of the two sets of notes constitutes proof of the Crown case in the absence of a satisfactory explanation from the applicants. I had always understood that the burden of proof remains on the prosecution throughout, but in any event one might ask what chance these applicants have of rebutting the allegations in the absence of the evidence I have just referred to. I would further comment that the delay in this case took place notwithstanding the fact that the file at the Surrey police headquarters was searched at the request of Armstrong's solicitors in July 1975; that the Director of Public Prosecutions had access to all documents in 1974 and 1975 and they were in the custody of the Avon and Somerset police from August 1987 to May 1989 when they were examined and the investigation began.

The defence have also raised the first limb of abuse of process. They say the prosecution have manipulated and misused the process of the court so as to deprive the defendants of a protection provided by the law. The defence point to the failure to caution the applicants and the failure to serve the required regulation 7 notices prior to those interviews or within a proper time. What gives the gravest concern is the explanation given by the officer in charge of the Avon and Somerset inquiry. Under cross-examination he had admitted that it was a deliberate policy decision not to caution any of these applicants before any of the interviews of which there were three in the case of Donaldson and Attwell and four in the case of Style. This was because to caution might encourage these three to exercise their right of silence. This was clearly a flagrant violation of the Police and Criminal Evidence Act. In consequence of a 'deliberate policy decision' these three men were kept in the dark as to the real intentions of the interviewers and deprived of a crucial right given to prospective defendants by the law of this country. The same may be said of regulation 7 notices, which should have been served as soon as possible, soon having been held to mean days rather than weeks. In my view these actions, which appear designed to conceal from the applicants the fact that they were under serious suspicion for grave crimes and thus deprived them of the opportunity to seek evidence from others who may have assisted their case, amounts to a denial of natural justice and, therefore, inevitably an abuse of the process of the court. My view on that aspect is greatly strengthened by the fact that these interviews took place only one month before the hearing in the Court of Appeal on October 18, 1989, following which there was a storm of denunciation of men against whom not a solitary word of evidence had been given in a court of law. Men who were uncharged, unheard, untried and unconvicted.

It is to that aspect of the case that I shall now turn. No complaint is made of objective reporting on television and in the press of matters which undoubtedly are of great public interest. The criticism is of those—and I do not propose to name anyone—who in a rush to judgment spoke of lies, perjury, concoction of evidence and corruption by the police officers involved in the interviews, as though the charges had already been proved. I have heard hours of television and read copious files of newspaper cuttings and have looked and listened in vain for the word 'alleged'. In the avalanche of condemnation it is not an exaggeration to say that the presumption of innocence, which applies to all persons accused of crime, including police officers, was turned into a presumption of guilt. Mr Justice Turner in the *Zeebrugge* case has made it clear that prejudice arising from media coverage is a factor to be considered in abuse of process. Can it be said that grave prejudice to men who must be presumed innocent does not arise from such headlines as 'Five cops in the frame'; 'The liars, bomb police fixed the evidence'; 'Guilty officers must be jailed, relatives say', and 'The bent copper', or an article by the author of a book on the subject, which is typical of many such comments–'We have now been told officially that what an increasing number of people had come to see as the truth over a period of 15 years *is indeed true*. The so-called confessions of the Guildford Four were the product of 'concoction and fabrication' on the part of that Surrey Constabulary which arrested and interrogated them and charged them with murder in 1974'. The further association of the officers in the Guildford Four case with those in the Birmingham Six has made the prejudice more protracted.

I have therefore come to the following conclusions:

The delay has been sufficiently extreme to raise a general inference of prejudice.

The specific disadvantages suffered by the defendants through lapse of time in the preparation of their case will prejudice them at their trial.

The adverse public comment through the media is highly prejudicial.

The failure to caution at the interviews was a misuse and a manipulation of the powers of the court.

> For the above reasons there has been an abuse of the process of the court in this case and the applicants are accordingly discharged."

As the result of this ruling I found that it was my turn to be in the eye of the storm. I was, quite wrongly, associated with all that had gone before in the *Guildford* case. The editor of the *Daily Mirror,* in an article in that newspaper of June 12, 1991, stated:

> "The innocence of the Guildford Four and the subsequent accusation that police had been involved in fabricating evidence struck right at the heart of the British judicial system and nipped at the fabric of our way of life. Yesterday Mr Ronald Bartle, a professional lawyer and magistrate, decided to dismiss the charges against the three policemen. He gave his reasons in an argument that we at the *Daily Mirror* think outrageous, disgraceful and a travesty of justice that will make Britain the laughing stock of the world."

I must confess it came as a surprise to me to learn that my influence was global, but since that announcement emanated from a newspaper which is not noted for the moderation of its tone I was less flattered than might otherwise have been the case. Had the criticisms to which I was subjected been less absurd I might have considered them worthy of reply, but they were so ludicrous that I lost not a wink of sleep. I was accused of dismissing the case against the police "without even hearing the evidence." In fact in an abuse of process application the tribunal concerned has to make its decision before evidence is called.

So incensed was Mr Chris Mullin, MP, at my ruling that he wrote to the Lord Chancellor asking for an assurance that I should not preside over committal proceedings arising out of the convictions of the Birmingham Six. In the letter Mr Mullin was quoted as saying (*Independent on Sunday,* October 27, 1991) "The point about Mr Bartle is that given his well-known views that police officers are incapable of wrongdoing he is an entirely inappropriate person to be dealing with cases of this kind."

Mr Mullin had fallen into error on several points. First, in this country, as in every genuine democracy, the judiciary is independent of the executive. He was enlightened on this subject in a reply from the Lord

Chancellor in which Lord Mackay stated that the government could not interfere with the independence of the courts. Secondly, we have a system of appeal by which higher courts correct errors made by those of inferior status. In fact this occurred in the *Guildford* police case. My ruling was overturned in the Divisional Court of the High Court of Justice. Thirdly, I have never been biased in favour of police officers as such. My ruling was based on well-established legal principles as I have already indicated. Fourthly, and finally, if Mr Mullin had been present in court at Bow Street some weeks after the *Guildford* case he would have heard my ruling in a similar application go against the police. In the course of that ruling I said,

"This court decides every case by applying the law to the facts before it. This court does not make law, it applies it. The higher courts make the law through decided cases. If I err in law the higher court will put me right. Police officers, when appearing as defendants in abuse of process applications, or any other proceedings, are treated exactly the same as anyone else. On such applications the court sometimes allows and sometimes disallows by reference to the law alone. There is no bias whatever, and to suggest that there is, is utter nonsense."

The Crown's appeal against my decision was heard on January 24, 1992. The Attorney General, Sir Patrick Mayhew, accepted on behalf of the Crown that the delay of about 18 years between the relevant interviews and the date when the trial could take place would inevitably result in some prejudice to the respondents. My other conclusions, however, he contended, were insupportable and such that no reasonable magistrate could have reached on the material before him. These submissions were upheld and my judgment was over-ruled. Consequently, the three defendants were committed for trial to the Old Bailey. It was there that the last act of this particular drama took place.

After a retirement of over eight hours the jury acquitted all three defendants on all charges. The Home Secretary at the time, Kenneth Clarke, was quoted as saying, "I think we should accept the verdict and should not just listen to the campaigners who had made up their minds a long time ago about what happened." It was of some interest to myself to study the press reaction to the jury's verdict. The *Daily Mirror* suddenly adopted a less strident tone: "No innocent person should be sent to prison, whether they are a police officer or a suspected terrorist." The *Guardian,* in reference to my own part in the proceedings, declared that I had played "a key role." This was yet another inaccuracy. I ruled on a point of law—that is all. Books have been written and even a film made about the *Guildford Four* case. I have read none of them nor have I seen the film. I make no pronouncement whatever on the case itself. The Court of Appeal ruled that their convictions were unsafe and could not be sustained and that is that.

But as far as the three police officers who were finally acquitted and exonerated are concerned, I believe that the monstrous campaign of vilification to which they were subjected by the press, by journalists and by many others who should have known better, to be an episode of surpassing disgrace and injustice.

CHAPTER 5

Security — Does it Exist?

When, some years ago, a young man fired shots at the Queen during the Trooping the Colour ceremony on Horseguards Parade, the country was reminded of the danger which always lurks in the wings for those who are the leading figures in public life. On that occasion Her Majesty was indeed fortunate. The shots which the assailant fired were blanks, but a subsequent search of his flat revealed literature on the subject of assassination, together with indications of target practice with live rounds. He appeared before me on committal at Bow Street, a smart young naval cadet in his late-twenties. He was charged with an offence under the Treason Act of putting the Sovereign in fear and was subsequently sentenced at the Old Bailey to a period of six years' imprisonment.

Yet there is nothing uniquely unusual for reigning sovereigns and other members of royalty to be subjected to violent attack. In 1800 an attempt was made on the life of George III when he was attending the theatre in Drury Lane. James Hadfield, a mentally unbalanced individual, fired at the king, but fortunately with defective aim. Hadfield was defended at his trial by the great advocate, Thomas Erskine, later to be Lord Chancellor, and acquitted on the grounds of insanity. The case became a landmark in the law of the criminal liability of persons of unsound mind. Queen Victoria was the victim of a similar attempt, again unsuccessful. In more recent times an armed man tried to abduct Princess Anne when her car was being driven up The Mall, and the murder of the Queen's cousin, Lord Mountbatten, by the IRA, is of recent memory.

Only one English Prime Minister has been assassinated while in office. Spencer Percival was shot down as he left the House of Commons one evening by a deranged man who suffered from imaginary grievances. Mrs Thatcher had a narrow escape at the Brighton hotel bombing and

Mr John Major was at a Cabinet meeting at No. 10 when an IRA mortar attack was made on the building.

There is, to the best of my knowledge, only one instance in modern times of a circuit judge being murdered by a man he had previously sentenced. There is no record of a stipendiary magistrate suffering such a fate, although an erstwhile colleague of mine, now deceased, was fired at when he was presiding on the bench. The bullet missed his head by a narrow margin. However, it is said that being elderly and somewhat deaf he was under the impression that somebody had dropped a book.

It has been said that it always seems to be the wrong people who are the victims of assassination. There would appear to be something in this view: Lincoln, Ghandi, Kennedy, Sadat, Rabin: these are names we associate with democracy, freedom and the pursuit of peace and conciliation. All fell to the hand of an assassin. Hitler, Stalin, Pol Pot: these were blood-stained tyrants yet they escaped such a fate. Hitler was the subject of a number of serious attempts on his life, all of which failed. He died eventually by his own hand.

Questions of security which arise at Bow Street frequently concern comparatively minor matters such as the lady who threw a pot of paint into the chamber of the House of Commons from the public gallery, the disturbance in the presence of the Queen Mother at the inaugural ceremony at the "Bomber" Harris statue and the trouble caused by a gatecrasher at the Royal Society of Arts shortly before the arrival of Prince Charles. In extradition cases, however, it is not uncommon for terrorist defendants to appear. These include mafia men, political extremists and of course, members of the IRA. The maximum security court was for a time situated near the Elephant and Castle, then in Arbour Square and finally at the court at Belmarsh Prison, near Woolwich, which has been especially constructed for the purpose.

For those whose profession it is to enforce the law there is an ever-present element of danger. It has been my pleasant duty from time-to-time as a Bow Street stipendiary to present awards to police officers for examples of great courage in carrying out their duties. The sum of money they receive is almost derisory by today's values, but the certificate for honourable conduct and bravery shown in the course of duty is, I am sure, greatly prized. Tackling an armed criminal without anything to defend oneself with save a truncheon requires heroism of a quite extraordinary kind. Under fire and sometimes wounded, police officers risk, and not infrequently lay down, their lives for a public which tends to take it for granted that this is what the police are paid for. When I read newspaper headlines such as "Public losing confidence in the police" I wonder if those people who are so ready to criticise ever consider the sacrifice of life and limb which every officer is sworn to make, if necessary, to protect the citizen from violent and dangerous men.

Yet the same spirit of selflessness has to be shown by judges and magistrates. We too are in the danger zone. Incidents of violent conduct in court have increased markedly over recent years. Court police officers have been largely replaced by staff supplied by security firms, and they have proved worthy successors to the court officers. Courts themselves are being constructed to minimise the security risks, with glass panels around the dock and a glass screen partition separating the public gallery from the well of the court. At Belmarsh, near Woolwich, a special security court has been created at which terrorists and other potentially dangerous defendants appear. It is a comfort to be escorted to one's taxi surrounded by armed police officers, but having been placed in the vehicle their sudden departure is more than a little disconcerting.

Yet the greatest problem in protecting the vulnerable relates not to public figures or the courts but to millions of the elderly and the unprotected throughout the country who are the constant victims of crime. The police do their best, but their task is well nigh impossible. The involvement of the citizen in the battle with crime only receives a very limited response. Neighbourhood Watch schemes have proved effective in some areas but anything in the nature of vigilantes is, understandably, opposed by the police. It is easier to protect property than to protect persons, but employing private security firms for this purpose can be expensive and well beyond the means of the poorer section of the community. This is where, in my view, there is a place for government assistance. It is the avowed policy of the government to cut back on the enormous, and in many instances unjustified level of, public expenditure, not only by extinguishing fraud, so far as this is possible, but by cutting back on welfare for those for whom it is either unrequired or undeserved. The sums thereby saved could then be directed to where they are really required. One such purpose, I would suggest, would be to enable the elderly who live alone and unprotected to secure their homes properly against the criminal intruder. It does seem an astonishing situation that thousands of illegal immigrants, "over-stayers" and the plainly workshy should be able to live month in month out on state benefit while nothing effective is done to relieve the nagging fears of old people that any day or night their homes may be broken into and they themselves subjected to horrific attack. I have to admit that the type of penalties which this author would consider appropriate for offenders of this kind are no longer on the statute book.

A further proposal would be the recruitment of unemployed young people to accompany the elderly and solitary on shopping trips in high crime areas of major cities, or in other similar situations. The two greatest social problems in our society today are surely the single parent and the lonely and unprotected elderly. A good deal has been done for the former, many of whom have acquired their status voluntarily; comparatively little for the latter. Children too are sometimes at risk to a degree never before experienced. But in their case the responsibility must rest with parents.

CHAPTER 6

Crime Knows No Frontiers

In January 1991, I was privileged to be invited to address the United Nations Asia and Far East Institute for the Suppression of Crime and Treatment of Offenders. I spoke on the subject of extradition, since this is the special Bow Street jurisdiction and a subject with which I had become familiar. As the world rapidly becomes a smaller place inter-state co-operation for the purpose of combatting international crime is increasingly important. The international criminal today is generally engaged in either drug-trafficking, the "laundering" of the proceeds of such activity, fraud on a global scale, or terrorism. Such criminals are greatly assisted by a number of factors. First, there is the speed and availability of modern transport, especially by air. Secondly, there is the technology of modern communication and information transmission such as the internet. Thirdly, there are the facilities for the transfer of huge sums of money across the world. Fourthly, the lack of inter-state policing arrangements (which are being improved gradually) leaves much to be desired. Fifthly, and most relevantly in the context of law, is the unsatisfactory state of extradition arrangements which remains the situation among certain countries. Finally, there is the hesitancy of some states to enter into or ratify convention agreements to facilitate the apprehension and return of fugitive offenders. Having outlined in my address the English law on the subject, I proposed what I felt were the steps which needed to be taken.

First, multilateral conventions are much to be preferred to bilateral treaties. In this way the net to trap fugitive criminals is spread much wider. Secondly, all states throughout the world should be parties to general agreements. Ad hoc arrangements are not satisfactory. Thirdly, conventions and treaties should seek to simplify extradition and extend facilities for the mutual provision of evidence between the parties. Fourthly, states should provide facilities for the law enforcement agents of other nations to follow criminals in "hot pursuit" into their jurisdiction with a minimum of protocol. Fifthly, extradition arrangements and the law applying thereto should seek to reduce to the minimum the chances of offenders avoiding justice on technicalities. Finally it should never be necessary to provide evidence of a *prima facie* case in hearings involving terrorists.

Since 1991 when I gave my address to the United Nations Asia and Far East Institute for the Prevention of Crime and the Treatment of Offenders (UNAFEI) in Tokyo, there has in fact been considerable progress on several of these points, though I may confidently assume that this is not the result of my speech. Firstly, under European Union provisions, communications between European police forces have been greatly improved. Secondly, technology for the interception of messages between one state and another has advanced considerably. Thirdly, there has been progress in the methods of identification of individuals at airports and other places of public transit. Fourthly, the records of known international criminals are up-to-date and remarkably comprehensive.

It is not my intention to depart from the spirit of this work by exhausting the reader with an account of United Kingdom extradition law. However, I feel obliged to say something about the role of the Bow Street magistrate when dealing with these cases in order to avoid the kind of misunderstanding which, as I have already indicated, arose in the field of abuse of process.

United Kingdom extradition law effectively dates from the Extradition Act 1870. Prior to this every treaty with a foreign state for the surrender of fugitive criminals required an Act of Parliament before effect could be given to it in this country. These old Acts were repealed by the Extradition Act 1870. Commonwealth countries were dealt with in the Fugitive Offenders Act 1881, until its repeal by the Fugitive Offenders Act 1967. The Extradition Act of 1989, which came into force on September 27, 1989, amended and consolidated the law in relation to extradition to foreign countries and the return of fugitives to countries in the Commonwealth.

The 1870 Act contained a list of extraditable offences. The requesting state, broadly speaking, had to satisfy the English court (Bow Street) that there was a treaty in existence, that an offence had been committed and the offence was a crime under the treaty and by the law of both countries. The Act of 1989 simplified the position by defining an extradition crime as one which is punishable in the United Kingdom with 12 months imprisonment or more.

In furtherance of greater facilitation and expedition of the return of criminals who seek a safe haven abroad, the European Convention was drawn up and opened for signature by the Council of Europe on December 13, 1957. This was signed, and subsequently ratified by a number of western European countries, together with one or two others outside Europe such as Turkey, Cyprus and Israel. The Convention was incorporated into English law on May 14, 1991. It brought about a very important change. Some of the basic requirements which previously applied were preserved: the documents had to be properly authenticated, the defendant correctly identified, the conduct an extradition offence under the 1989 Act and by the law of the requesting state before which the fugitive was an accused or convicted person. But it is no longer necessary, when the requesting state is a party to the Convention, for that state to establish to the magistrate's satisfaction that there is enough evidence to found a *prima facie* case. There are now therefore three systems in operation: extradition to Convention countries, to non-Convention countries and to Commonwealth nations.

A final point to mention is that the United Kingdom has made several reservations to the Convention. We do not extradite persons who have been convicted *in absentia,* who are the subject of criminal proceedings for the crime in question in this country or who have already been convicted or acquitted of that offence. Moreover extradition may not be ordered where there has been an unjust lapse of time, or if the fugitive will be tried for other offences besides those for which extradition is sought or where to extradite would prejudice an existing treaty. The Convention is consistent with existing United Kingdom law in that extradition is not to be ordered for political or military offences and a state can refuse to extradite if to do so would result in the death penalty.

It is important to mention that the role of the Bow Street magistrate in extradition proceedings is as near as may be to that of a court of committal for trial in a domestic criminal case. If the case is a non-Convention one the magistrate must be satisfied that there is a *prima facie* case. If it is a Convention hearing the basic requirements already outlined must be satisfied. But it is not the magistrate who extradites. He or she commits the defendant to await the direction of the Secretary of State. Thus the final decision is an executive, not a judicial one. The Home Secretary retains a discretion as to whether or not to act upon the magistrate's order.

In September 1995 there came before me one of the most extraordinary examples of international computer crime it would be possible to imagine. Standing in the dock was a young man named Vladimir Levin. He was 28 years-of-age, and, as the name would indicate, was a Russian. In appearance he could have been a student of the more serious academic type. In fact he was a computer hacker accused of employing his technical skills to try to steal £8 million from one of the world's largest banks. He had been arrested in this country having been unwise enough to leave his native St Petersburg. The United States of America were seeking his committal to that country where he was wanted by the FBI for his part in a worldwide "sting" against the American-owned Citicorp, which he conducted from an office in St Petersburg. Quite simply the defendant, who had been employed in a small trading company in St Petersburg, unknown to his employers and using a £700 desktop personal computer, had "hacked" into the computer of Citibank N A in Parsippanny, New Jersey, and made transfers of money from the accounts of unsuspecting victims into various bank accounts around the world which were controlled by him and his associates. Levin, who had acquired the requisite password and user identification codes was assisted by a confederate who, after the wire-transfers had been effected, collected the money from each of the banks to which it had been sent. The matter came to light when a bank employee stared at his computer screen in astonishment to see money being siphoned from legitimate accounts to new accounts in San Francisco. The criminal associate, who was arrested on his next visit posing as a "customer," gave evidence on behalf of the

United States government. The FBI discovered that Citicorp's supposedly impregnable computer system had been hacked into 40 times in five months. This was a new dimension of theft and one which sent a shudder through the world of international commerce and finance. The case, like a number of other extradition hearings in which I have given a ruling, went on appeal to the House of Lords on one or two interesting points of law which I will mention but briefly.

The defendant faced a number of charges which fell into three groups: theft, offences under the Computer Misuse Act and forgery and false accounting. Mr Alun Jones, QC, a leading counsel in this field, submitted that there was no theft at the time alleged in the charges, namely when the money was collected from the bogus accounts in various banks, because appropriation, an essential ingredient in the crime of theft, had already taken place when the wire-transfers were made. On this point I held that the transfers were merely preparatory to appropriation and therefore part of a chain of events culminating in the real or final theft. It was further submitted by the defence that the computer printouts were inadmissible because they were hearsay. In criminal proceedings, it was argued, they would be admissible under section 69 of the Police and Criminal Evidence Act 1984, but extradition proceedings had been held not to be criminal proceedings. In the subsequent appeal, in an important judgment Lord Hoffman said:

> "The printouts were tendered to prove the transfers of funds which they recorded. They recorded the transfers themselves, created by the interaction between whoever purported to request the transfers and the computer. The evidential status of the printouts is no different from that of a photocopy of a forged cheque."

Most significantly the learned Law Lord stated: "Extradition proceedings are criminal proceedings. They are of course criminal proceedings of a very special kind, but they are criminal proceedings nonetheless." Vladimir Levin was duly extradited to the United States.

Another extraordinary case it fell to my lot to decide also involved computers, although this was not extradition and the defendant, though young, indeed younger than Levin, was a schoolboy aged 16. In order to avoid embarrassment to his family, I will call him Raymond. It came as a great shock to Raymond's thoroughly respectable family when suddenly one evening in May 1994 the police entered their house in considerable numbers and burst into Raymond's room. There they searched for five hours, after which they took away a computer and other items. Raymond's mother was quoted as saying: "We never thought this would go to court. He was just a kid messing about on his computer." That was in fact a very considerable understatement. What her son had in fact succeeded in doing was to hack into the United States Air Force defence systems. There was panic at the Pentagon. Military chiefs believed that an east European spy ring was stealing their secrets. Senate hearings were told that the West faced a new type of electronic enemy who was doing more harm than the KGB. Investigations took 13 months to track the source of the intrusion to England at an estimated cost of £250,000 while the American Air Force spent hundreds of thousands of dollars reviewing and tightening its security systems.

The culprit was a mild-mannered and obviously likeable young man whose real gifts lay in the field of music, not computers. The prosecution had taken a considerable time to be brought to court and the defendant was 19 when he finally appeared before me at Bow Street in March 1997 charged with 12 offences under the Computer Misuse Act.

It was said by the prosecution that possibly the most serious episode was when he hacked into the computer of a Korean atomic research institute. America was then conducting delicate negotiations with the North Koreans and the negotiators were greatly alarmed at the prospect of being accused of an aggressive action. It appeared that the break-in came from a United States air base. In the event Raymond admitted 12 offences under the Computer Misuse Act and was fined a total of £1,200. He left the court determined to confine his energies to his music, at which he will no doubt excel as he did with his computer activities, but with far happier consequences.

One of the most tragic events in the world of banking occurred with the collapse of the Bank of Credit and Commerce International, a vast organization which controlled a world-wide network of banks and financial institutions. That crash, which was brought about by fraud and not by market forces, meant ruin for thousands of small account holders who, until then, believed that their hard-earned savings were in safe hands. Anyone who saw on their television screen the distraught faces of people who despairingly attempted to effect entry to the banks to withdraw their savings could not fail to be incensed over the villainy which had brought the situation about. The Bank of England was criticised at the time for being slow to wake up to the situation and to alert depositors to their peril before it was too late. Whether this criticism was justified or not I cannot say, but had an observer from that great financial institution been present in my court during an extradition hearing in March 1998, they would very quickly have had their eyes opened to the criminal and corrupt activities with which BCCI was riddled from top to bottom.

The case involved conspiracy to "launder" the proceeds of drug-trafficking which was, as is well known, taking place between Columbia and major cities in the United States of America. The defendant was manager of the Paris branch of BCCI. Other branches of that same bank in both America and Europe had been targeted by the conspirators for a similar purpose. The United States government was requesting the extradition of the defendant to that country on six charges of entering into arrangements to launder the proceeds of drug-trafficking, conspiracy to possess cocaine with intent to supply to others and conspiracy to evade restrictions on importation of cocaine into the United States. I will not weary the reader with the details of what were very complicated and protracted transactions. I shall deal with them fairly briefly. The key witnesses for the prosecution, indeed virtually the only witnesses, were two American under-cover customs agents. Posing as drug-traffickers they insinuated themselves into the discussions and dealings of the conspirators This is work which, it goes without saying, is not only delicate and difficult, but also extremely dangerous for the agents. On this occasion they were highly successful. One of the agents, pretending to be a man of substantial business interests, met up with a known Columbian drug trafficker and successfully persuaded the Columbian to accept himself and his fellow agent as genuine recruits to the operation. An account was opened at the Panama City branch of BCCI. In order to fund this account the proceeds of cocaine sales were transferred via other branches of BCCI in the USA. An officer of BCCI Panama who was also involved in the scheme, warned of its unsatisfactory nature and suggested a more sophisticated plan by which funds would be wired from the United States to a foreign branch of BCCI in a country with strict secrecy laws. From there the funds would be wired directly to accounts in Columbia. A further meeting took place at BCCI Miami at which one of the main participants recommended that BCCI Luxembourg be used. Finally, however, the branch in Paris was settled on as the centre of operations. The agents were told that Paris would be happy to do whatever they wanted.

There followed a series of discussions between the under-cover agents and the defendant who was regional manager of BCCI for Europe and Africa. These conversations were monitored on tape recorders which were in the briefcases of the agents. On the basis of those recordings the case for the government of the United States was founded. That case was that the defendant was told by the under-cover agents that they wished to conduct financial transactions via BCCI Paris with funds that were the proceeds from cocaine sales in the United States made by the under-cover agents' Columbian clients, and that the defendant agreed to do so. It was said that the defendant, with the assistance of his subordinates, who also had knowledge that the funds resulted from drug transactions in the United States, arranged for bank accounts to be opened at the BCCI Paris branch on behalf of the under-cover agents and their Columbian clients. The defendant met with the Columbian clients in the presence of the under-cover agents and provided the clients with information relating to BCCI to induce the Colombians to do business with BCCI. The scheme agreed upon was that proceeds from cocaine sales in the United States were to be wire transferred to bank accounts at BCCI Paris which were controlled by the agents and/or the Columbian clients and placed in certificates of deposit. These funds were to be either wire transferred to other accounts controlled by the under-cover agents or the Colombians or used as collateral for the granting of loans to individuals or entities designated and controlled by the Colombians. Regardless of the method, those funds would be thereby returned to the

Columbian clients in a manner which would disguise the nature, location, source and ownership of the funds as well as enable the clients to continue cocaine-trafficking activities in the United States.

The defendant, it was claimed, participated directly in two transactions. The first in May 1988, involved the wire transfer of $1,000,000 in cocaine proceeds which was part of a larger sum delivered to under-cover agents in the United States by unindicted co-conspirators in April 1988. This sum was wire transferred to BCCI Paris, placed in a deposit account and in July 1988 transferred to BCCI Panama. The second transaction involved the transfer of a sum of similar size derived from cocaine proceeds via BCCI Luxembourg to BCCI Paris and thence to BCCI Panama.

The apprehension of the conspirators was achieved by a "sting" operation which was not without its comic aspect. A male and a female under-cover agent announced their engagement and invited their co-conspirators to their "wedding" in Miami on October 10. That happy occasion was interrupted by the arrival of armed police officers and the guests entered into bonds, but not those of matrimony. The defendant however, possibly having "smelt a rat" did not attend but instead came to England where his attendance at Court No.1, Bow Street, proved a less congenial occasion than a wedding reception. He was in due course extradited.

A number of colourful characters appeared before me at Bow Street. One such was Azil Nadir. Mr Nadir, charged in connection with his dealings with his company, Polly Peck, was desirous of a modification of his bail conditions to facilitate visits to Northern Cyprus in connection with his business activities. I declined the application — but he left anyway. Another was Mr Ronnie Knight who passed through my court on his way from the sunny Costa del Sol to the distinctly less congenial package vacation offered by Bow Street to its guests.

A case with shades of *Spycatcher* was that of Richard Tomlinson. Mr Tomlinson, who had been dismissed by MI6 in 1995, was charged under section 1(1) of the Official Secrets Act which makes it an offence for a former intelligence officer to divulge sensitive information acquired in that capacity. It was said by the prosecution that a deal was agreed between the defendant and his former employers under the terms of which he would drop his claim for unfair dismissal and hand over all the information he had written down, both on paper and on his computer. Notwithstanding this, it was said, the defendant had been in negotiation with a firm of publishers in Sydney, Australia and had offered a seven-page synopsis and short preface outlining the first seven chapters. Mr Tomlinson pleaded guilty to a charge under section 1 and was committed for sentence to the Old Bailey.

CHAPTER 7

Magistrates: Lay and Stipendiary

Since the advent of the Labour Government in 1997, important developments have begun to take place which, if continued, may effect a very great change in the magistracy of this country, lay and stipendiary. In the course of this chapter I would like to assess the degree of change which may be anticipated and to comment, on the basis of 27 years' experience of the bench, on whether I see the likely consequences to be for the better or for the worse. It is not my wish to sound controversial. Here we are in the realm of law, not politics. It is in the interest of every law-abiding citizen, magistrates included, that the nation enjoys a system of justice which is efficient, fair and adapted to the times in which we live. It is in the nature of the British people that they prefer change to be evolutionary, not revolutionary, and no doubt that is how things will continue to be done in this country. But change there must always be, and it is a matter of amazement how many causes which today appear to us as inherently just and sensible once had to be fought for against bitter and powerful opposition. One only has to mention the abolition of the slave-trade, the universal franchise and the emancipation of women to name but three. It is also true to say that the introduction of a professional police force as well as the creation of the stipendiary magistrate met with fierce opposition at the time. In a free society the future shape of its institutions can never be regarded as non-negotiable.

A second point I would like to emphasise is that any opinion I express is entirely my own. Naturally, as a stipendiary magistrate, my views are coloured by the obvious interest on my part to see the well-being and status of the body to which I belong upheld and advanced. But I entertain no contrary bias or prejudice where the lay justices are concerned and any observations I may make which may appear to be critical relate to the system and not to individuals.

The justices of the peace are a body of ladies and gentlemen of wholly admirable qualities. They are selected by the Lord Chancellor on the basis of uprightness of character, lively and well-balanced intellect and a wholesome desire to commit themselves to a form of public service which has no superior—the administration of justice. This they do without material reward and in the knowledge that they must sacrifice a good deal of time which they could otherwise devote to their private lives. There is no other country in the world which can boast such a worthy body of non-professional judicial officers. If there is to be some modification of their present role in the judicial system, that is due to changes of many kinds in society and is no adverse reflection on the justices themselves.

The office of justice of the peace has its roots embedded in the distant past. In the 13th century *custodes pads* or keepers of the peace, were established whose duty it was "to arrest all malefactors and keep them in safe custody awaiting orders from the Crown." It is interesting to note that from the earliest time JPs were entrusted with administrative as well as judicial duties and this was so for hundreds of years until the modern era when their function became judicial only (excepting licensing matters which are virtually all that is left of their administrative powers). Their importance increased following disorders which arose due to the return of unruly soldiers from foreign wars and the widespread unrest resulting from the depopulation of the country caused by the Black Death. The Justices of the Peace Act of 1361, however, is generally regarded as establishing the office of JP on a permanent basis, and the Act described the scope of the office as follows:

> "In every county of England shall be assigned for the keeping of the peace, one Lord and with him three or four of the most worthy in the county, with some learned in the law and they shall have power to restrain the offenders, rioters and all other barrators [exciters of quarrels] and to pursue, arrest, take and chastise them according to their trespass and offence...and to inquire of all those who have been pillors [pillagers] and robbers in the parts beyond the sea, and be now come again, and go wandering, and will

not labour as they were wont in times past; and to take and arrest all those that they may find by indictment, or by suspicion, and to put them in prison, and to take all of them that be not of good fame where they shall be found, sufficient surety…of the good behaviour towards the King and his people, and the others duly to punish; to the intent that the people be not by rioters or rebels troubled nor endamaged, nor the peace blemished…and also to hear and determine at the King's suit all manner of felonies and trespasses done in the same county, according to the laws and customs aforesaid."

Two significant features of this early piece of legislation affecting magistrates are worthy of note. First, the powers it bestows are far in excess of those which magistrates possess today. Secondly, it contains the power to bind a defendant over to be of good behaviour, a form of disposal which still survives to this day.

Foreigners are frequently astonished that people with no formal legal training or qualifications should sit in judgment on their fellows. The system of a lay judiciary is unknown in Europe as it is elsewhere in the world outside the Commonwealth. It is also the case that judges in the lower courts on the continent frequently take part in the investigative process, while the higher judiciary carry out much of the questioning during the trial which in an English court is performed by counsel. Yet there is something about the nature of the lay magistracy which, like the jury system, has its roots deep in the English character. We do not like our lives being governed from the cradle to the grave by officials. We feel affection for the amateur, although there is now a growing tendency away from this. As Edward Grierson points out in his book *Confessions of a Country Magistrate:*

> "Reformers, impatient with the anomalies of a lay Magistracy, have suggested abolishing the lay justices altogether. This is a view in line with modern thinking which in almost every sphere is intolerant of the amateur. We see it even in sport. To be 'professional' in one's work is now the highest praise. To hand over the benches in England and Wales to a paid Magistracy would, it is argued, certainly make for efficiency and prevent the errors and misjudgments to which laymen are subject when they tres-

pass on technical ground. No one, however, has ever troubled to analyse or evaluate these lapses which do occur in the course of the justices' work as they occur in every field of human activity, however professional. The low rate of successful appeals against decisions of the justices, on which we have already remarked, suggests in fact that they do their work well rather than badly—their failure rate is probably no higher than that of surgeons, physicians, barristers, solicitors, Judges, engineers and experts of all kinds."

Another criticism levelled against magistrates is the discrepancy in sentencing which occurs between one court and another. It sometimes happens that in one court a heavier fine is imposed for a driving offence than that which is inflicted in another for a crime of violence. A programme of seminars and conferences has been organized for magistrates to introduce as far as possible conformity of sentencing. Yet human factors always ensure disparity of approach. Surveys of sentences passed in different areas of the country illustrate this. The great weakness inherent in these sort of statistics is the fact that one is told nothing of the circumstances of the offences, the antecedents of the offenders or factors in mitigation. It is for precisely the same reasons that newspaper reports on this subject can be so totally misleading. In comparing one sentence with another the reporter omits to mention important considerations which had led the bench to their decision. This may well be because there is simply not enough space for a full description of the case, or it may, of course, be due to the fact that one-sided reporting makes more arresting reading than an impartial account. Generally speaking, the standard of justice administered by JPs is high. There is no convincing argument for their abolition.

There is, however, an argument for their replacement on a limited scale by stipendiaries. This is because of the far greater speed with which stipendiary magistrates get through the work. There were two basic reasons for the creation of salaried magistrates. The first was the necessity, in early-19th century London, for a body of professionals on the bench to cope with the growing volume of crime in the metropolis. The second concerned the conduct of the justices of the time whose behaviour, in sharp contrast to the ladies and gentlemen who fulfil these functions

Magistrates: Lay and Stipendiary

today, left much to be desired. In rural areas, the principal criticism of the magistrates was directed not so much at their venality as at their inefficiency and their authoritarian behaviour. After the horrific "Peterloo Massacre" of 1819, the magistrates responsible for setting the military on peaceful demonstrators were termed "ignorant petty tyrants." Since eleven innocent protesters were killed in that outrage, the term could hardly be considered unjust.

The element of financial corruption was exposed by a committee of inquiry established in 1814 for the purpose of looking into the administration of the county of Middlesex over the preceding 20 years. Yet strange to say, notwithstanding these scandals, there was opposition both inside and outside Parliament to the concept of the professional magistracy, as indeed there was a short while later to the establishment of a professional police force. It was thought that a salaried magistrate, acting alone without colleagues with whom to consult, and deciding guilt or innocence without the benefit of a jury, would be vulnerable to influence by the executive. It all seemed too continental in approach. Sydney Smith asked:

> "What in truth could we substitute for the unpaid Magistracy? We have no doubt but that a set of rural Judges, in the pay of the government, would very soon become corrupt jobbers and odious tyrants as they often are on the continent."

Happily that gloomy prophecy has not been fulfilled.

Something of a half-way house was established between the lay bench and stipendiaries as they are today with the establishment of the seven Public Offices at the turn of the century. These "magistrates of police" were paid £400 a year until 1821 when this was increased to £600 and in 1825 to £800 per annum. The Bow Street magistrates received the same salaries as the police magistrates, but Bow Street Court was never officially incorporated with the Public Offices.

There are several important differences between these early stipendiaries and those of today. First, the term "police magistrate" unashamedly identified the stipendiaries with the forces of law and order to an extent which would be thought undesirable today. Indeed, it was only in comparatively recent times that the metropolitan courts ceased to be designated "police courts." Secondly, the extraordinary hours which magistrates worked would be unthinkable now. The Fieldings often sat late into the night. A 15-hour day was not unusual. Thirdly, there was no statutory retirement age. Some magistrates remained on the bench until they were into their 80s, much to the chagrin of their critics.

Between 1812 and 1839 vacancies among the police magistrates were filled by the selection of barristers of at least three years standing. The Metropolitan Police Courts Act of 1839 firmly established the stipendiaries as a branch of the judiciary rather than the magistracy. It required at least seven years' practice at the Bar to qualify for the post and raised the salary to £1,200 a year and to £1,400 for the Chief Metropolitan Magistrate. Unlike their provincial brethren, the metropolitan stipendiaries were created to supplant rather than supplement the lay justices in those courts in which they were appointed to serve. The provincials were instituted in consequence of the influx of population into the manufacturing areas from 1760 onwards. After 1835 any borough (council) could petition the Home Secretary for the services of a stipendiary magistrate. Others were appointed by means of local Acts of Parliament.

Having provided this thumbnail sketch of the historical development of the stipendiary bench, let me now turn to the situation today.

Stipendiary magistrates consist of metropolitans and provincials, which in total amount to some 90 in all throughout the country. Their judicial status is, and always has been, somewhat anomalous. On the one hand they are termed "magistrates" and they sit in magistrates' courts administering justice at magisterial level. Yet they are at the same time professional salaried judges, sentencing and deciding guilt or innocence while sitting alone and consulting with nobody except themselves. This latter feature of their work makes the stipendiaries in some ways the most powerful judges in the land. Joshua Rozenburg refers to this in his book *The Search for Justice* (p. 129):

> "The vast majority of criminal cases—more than 93%—are heard in some 600 magistrates' courts throughout England and Wales. There are no juries.

Lay magistrates normally sit in benches of two or three while stipendiaries always sit alone.

Although there are limits to the sentence that magistrates may pass, they are the sole Judges of fact and law; in that sense a single Stipendiary has greater powers than a High Court Judge (who is bound by the jury's verdict on questions of fact) or an appeal Judge (who may be out voted by his or her colleagues)."

Over recent years the lay magistracy has in fact increased its influence. There are several reasons for this. First, the lay bench, unlike the stipendiary, is represented by a powerful national body, the Magistrates' Association, which has considerable influence at the highest levels of government and state. Secondly, the quality of lay magistrates has greatly improved in the last two or three decades due to the rigorous selection of appropriate candidates by the Lord Chancellor's Advisory Committees. Thirdly, the training programmes which justices must attend both before and subsequent to their appointment has given them a degree of knowledge which they did not possess in years past. Many years ago stipendiaries sat alone in the juvenile courts in the central London area. They were joined by lay justices, who now sit in the family and youth courts. Before 1971 JPs sat in Quarter Sessions on appeals from petty sessions. These took the form of re-trial without a jury. In the counties appeals were heard by the Appeal Committee of Quarter Sessions. In boroughs the recorder heard appeals alone, except when they were appeals from juvenile courts, when the recorder sat with two justices who were members of the juvenile panel. Justices also sat on committals for sentence and trials.

The Royal Commission on Assizes and Quarter Sessions 1966–1969 recommended that justices continue to be associated with the work of the new Crown Court, as assessors for useful training. This proposal was opposed by the Magistrates' Association which wished to retain full membership of the Crown Court bench. This was agreed by the then Lord Chancellor and his successor provided that the justices could give sufficient time to the work of the new circuit courts. Due to the increased work of the Crown Courts, a great many lay justices became involved in the judicial scene at this level. Section 74(1) of the Supreme Court Act 1981 provides that on

> "any hearing by the Crown Court of any appeal or of proceedings on committal to the Crown Court for sentence the Crown Court shall consist of a Judge of the High Court or a Circuit Judge or a Recorder who…shall sit with not less than two nor more than four Justices of the Peace."

By way of contrast, the status of the stipendiary bench has singularly failed to improve during the last quarter of a century. This was symbolised by the fact that the knighthood, traditional to the office of Chief Metropolitan Stipendiary Magistrate, and at one time conferred on appointment, was being awarded after a longer and longer period of service, and in the most recent instance, after retirement. This honour, which was originally intended to distinguish the importance of the position while the holder was in office, had become a leaving present. Secondly, the annual salary of a stipendiary magistrate, which in earlier days had been the same as that of a county court judge, fell further and further behind the income of the new circuit judges. The fact that stipendiaries became eligible for appointment to the circuit bench seemed to emphasise the implication that the Metropolitan bench is an inferior body whose members comprise those who have failed to qualify for promotion to the circuit bench. I am speaking from first-hand experience when I say that these developments brought about considerable lowering of morale among my colleagues on the Metropolitan bench.

The stipendiary magistrates have a reasonable desire that their special professionalism be recognised. This does not derive from a feeling of innate superiority over their lay brethren, but is based on a natural wish that their professional knowledge and qualifications should be employed to the best possible effect. Those aspirations have now begun to be fulfilled.

The Royal Commission on Criminal Justice, under the chairmanship of Viscount Runciman of Doxford, CBE, FBA, delivered in July 1998 its report to Parliament. Recommendation 255 declared: "There should be a more systematic approach to the role of Stipendiary Magistrates in the system to make best use of their special skills and qualifications." Subsequent developments would seem to indicate that this recommendation, emanating from such an important body, alerted the government to the fact that the potential of the stipendiary magistrate was not being fully realised. Consequently, in September 1994, the Lord Chancellor, with the agreement of the Lord Chief Justice, established a working party with the following terms of reference:

> "To produce, for the Lord Chancellor's consideration, a report containing guidelines identifying more clearly the respective roles of the Stipendiary Magistracy and the lay Bench in the administration of justice in the magistrates' court, having due regard to the differences between the needs of the shire counties and the metropolitan areas."

In the introduction to its report the working party distances itself from the more extreme views sometimes expressed by a minority on either side of the division separating the professional and lay magistrates:

> "We are...aware that there are some members of the lay Bench who are philosophically opposed to the appointment of Stipendiary Magistrates because, they believe, it is inimical to the interests of justice that one person should determine both issues of guilt and sentence. Likewise, there are some Stipendiaries who believe that the interests of justice might best be served only by the use of legally qualified professional magistrates. There are also some who fear that the increasing number of Stipendiary appointments made in recent years has had, or will have, the effect of removing interesting work from the lay Bench and that the Lord Chancellor harbours a secret intention to reduce the role and number of lay magistrates by appointing more Stipendiary Magistrates. In this last regard we pause only to observe that the Lord Chancellor has said, on very many occasions, that such is not his policy."

In its summary of recommendations the working party emphasised the partnership aspect of the joint work of the stipendiary and lay benches:

"The working party is of the view that the best use will only be made of a Stipendiary's special skills and qualifications where he or she works in partnership with, and is accepted by, the local community of lay magistrates."

The question of appointing more stipendiaries in the country at large was not within the terms of reference of the working party, but the issue was addressed, and rejected, in a Home Office publication of February, 1997, entitled "Review of Delay in the Criminal Justice System" (p.25 — More Stipendiaries?):

"A number of people suggested to me that the answer lay in the total or very substantial replacement of the lay Magistracy by stipendiaries. There is no doubt, based on the opinion of almost all court users, but also from my own observations, that stipendiaries are vastly more effective in managing the parties in any given case. The suggestion that there should be a significant increase in the number of stipendiaries is sometimes dismissed on cost grounds. I have not, in the time available, been able to carry out any sort of cost-benefit analysis, but I suspect the financial case for more stipendiaries is rather more in the balance than might be assumed. It is not, therefore, for financial reasons that I have rejected the possibility of a substantial increase in the numbers or proportion of stipendiaries. I have done so rather in recognition of the widespread and firmly held belief that the existence of the lay Magistracy is intrinsic to our justice system; because the Lord Chancellor has made his commitment to lay magistrates abundantly clear; but also because lay magistrates are, in my view, key to the success of efforts to retain more business in the magistrates' court. Certainly I think my proposals on removing the right of election for trial would be rather more difficult were the only alternative to Crown Court trial to be a hearing in front of a single Stipendiary."

The tenor of these conclusions would seem to be somewhat inconsistent with recommendation 31 in Annex A:

"Stipendiary Magistrates should be able to sit alone in the youth court and should specialise in the management of particularly complex cases."

The point regarding cost-effectiveness remained a factor for a government committed to seeking economies in the administration of justice. An investigation carried out by Leeds University claimed that in terms of expedition one stipendiary magistrate can get through the work of 30 lay justices in a comparable period of time, and with the cost of running 100 magistrates' courts in England and Wales now amounting to £260 million a year and rising, the present (1999) government undoubtedly feels this is a matter which should be grasped. In fact stipendiaries were already being employed on a wider basis throughout the country. This has been effected by an increase in the number of provincial stipendiaries, and also by a far greater use of "flying stipes," professional magistrates being sent to county and provincial courts to deal with cases of gravity or complexity which are not appropriately tried by the local bench. Moreover, while it is certainly true that the present government does not favour the wholesale replacement of lay justices by stipendiaries, it seems clear that the Home Secretary and the Lord Chancellor are leaning towards a greater degree of professionalisation of the magistracy.

In a Ministerial statement in 1998 Lord Irvine of Lairg, the Lord Chancellor, emphasised the professional status of the stipendiaries, stating "they are professional Judges." Two developments would seem to be essential if the programme of the present government is to be fulfilled.

The first is the establishment of the stipendiary bench as a nation-wide institution, similar, in that regard, to the circuit bench. This will involve as a preliminary the unification of the Metropolitan and provincial stipendiaries—a process which is already under way. The second is the unequivocal recognition of the stipendiary as a member of the judiciary, not the magistracy. In pursuance of this a change of title is clearly necessary. A judicial title ought to replace a magisterial one. The appearance in very recent times of the district judges, who were formerly County Court registrars, would indicate an obvious title: district judge. This has now been embodied in the Access to Justice Act 1999.

I am convinced that change of the kind dealt with above is an essential and inevitable part of the evolution of our system of justice, that it represents no threat to the lay magistracy and that once in place any misunderstanding and concern that may have arisen will be rapidly dispersed.

The most recent clarification of the position is the Access to Justice Act, which embodies as clear government policy the recognition of the professionalism of the stipendiary magistrates. The stipendiary bench is to be a national body in which the previous distinction between the metropolitan and provincial stipendiaries is abolished, thus forming one single new tier of the judiciary. Although the details have still to be settled, stipendiary magistrates will be eligible to sit in any court in the country if it is a court in which a stipendiary would normally preside if he or she has been specially designated by the chief magistrate to try a particular case. The second significant feature of the Bill in the magisterial context is the renaming of stipendiaries as district judge (magistrates' courts). Thus there will be one district bench neatly forming a third tier to the High Court and circuit benches.

It has to be said that these changes are not to the liking of the Magistrates' Association. That body has always been ultra-sensitive towards any developments which it considers may be prejudicial to the lay justices. It is the view of this author that sensitivity is excessive and unjustified. The association moved an amendment during the Bill through Parliament, to retain the original title of stipendiary magistrate, but I understand that this has been withdrawn. Nevertheless, a completely incomprehensible (to me) opposition to a perfectly reasonable proposal can exhibit itself in other ways.

There are areas of the country in which the incidence of crime is such as to more than merit the appointment of a stipendiary magistrate, yet the local lay bench are resistant to this taking place. Where such an appointment has been insisted upon by the Lord Chancellor the conditions which the prospective appointee has to meet are demeaning in the extreme. The plain fact is that the lay bench must accept with good grace the new situation. Only on that basis lies the way forward for the restructured judiciary.

CHAPTER 8

These I Have Known

In my early years at the Bar my practice was very largely in the London magistrates' courts. Most of my work at that time consisted of small criminal cases, in which I invariably defended. In those days I appeared in a great many Poor Persons cases, instructed by the Mary Ward Settlement. The Mary Ward, in Tavistock Place in the Bloomsbury area of London, was staffed by young barristers and solicitors who gave freely of their services in order to help those disadvantaged people who were not in a position financially to instruct a solicitor in the usual way. As advocates we represented our somewhat impecunious clients for a nominal fee. While our clients enjoyed the benefit of professional advice and representation virtually free of charge, we fledgling lawyers gained invaluable experience in advocacy.

In those early days, doing the round of London courts, I appeared before many of the stipendiaries of that generation whose names, although now largely forgotten, were once familiar to Londoners reading the columns of their evening newspapers. I think that the London "stipes" of that period were far more distinctive figures than those of today. There were several reasons for this. In those post-war years men whose practices had been interrupted by the war were content to accept an appointment at a modest judicial level which ensured a steady income and a pension on retirement. In most cases they had held commissioned rank and possessed the self-confidence which a degree of command had given them. There were fewer of them than is the case today and their connection with the lay justices was more tenuous. In addition to these factors it should be noted that magistrates at that time were less likely to be the subject of criticism by civil rights organizations for their sentencing, and had much less to fear from being reported and reprimanded for untoward comments made on the bench.

Yet, while some of them were regarded as "characters," they were far from being figures of fun. They were men with great experience of life — the average age was well above that of present day stipendiaries — and they discharged their judicial duties with a practical, down-to-earth competence. They did, however, differ greatly from each other in personality, as I discovered when I appeared in their courts.

There are people in this world who are extremely talented and who make a solid contribution to the society in which they live. Yet because they happen to possess a modest disposition and shun the limelight, or they excel in an area of life which makes little impact on the public scene, they achieve neither fame nor honours. By the same token, there are those whose talents are very limited, but because they have a gift for self-advancement and self-advertisement they receive a greater degree of recognition than their abilities merit. The modern media presents unrivalled opportunities for the second type. Geoffrey Rose fell firmly into the first category.

Rose sat at Lambeth Court and his quiet, considerate manner made it a pleasure to appear before him. No doubt by the standards of the raucous, strident society in which we now live such qualities are not at a premium, yet Rose was a man of remarkable gifts. I cannot do better than quote the words of his clerk, Stanley French, who, writing in his book *Crime Every Day* says this of Rose:

> "Truly it could be said of him that everything he touched he adorned. He won prizes at Harrow; some of them are on my shelves now. He was a scholar at King's, Cambridge, in 1908, a Foundation Scholar two years later. He got first-class honours in part 1 of the History Tripos, second-class honours in the Law Tripos, and a first-class and a certificate of honour in the Bar final examination…His military career was as distinguished as his scholastic career. He was awarded the MC and Bar and was twice mentioned in dispatches."

In addition to these attainments Rose had an extraordinary range of interests. He was a highly accomplished artist in watercolours, played the piano and wrote a regimental history illustrated with his own drawings. He studied botany and genealogy. At sport too he excelled. He played cricket, golf and lawn tennis and obtained medals for ice-skating. At 60 he took up advanced ballroom dancing in which he also received medals!

Another of the well-known London "beaks" of those days was Harold Sturge. I always found it a pleasure to appear before Sturge because, like Rose, he was a benign tribunal from the point of view of the advocate. Sturge was one of those magistrates who endeavour to exercise a good influence by means of the office they occupy. A naturally kind man he was compassionate in the administration of justice. I liked to hear him address defendants in the manner of an understanding uncle. He gave fresh hope to those who had fallen low in life. In domestic disputes he would speak words of reconciliation where this was appropriate. He sat for most of his time at Old Street Court, later on moving to South West Court at Clapham. He wrote several books about the law, and like Rose, was an accomplished amateur artist. Appointed to the bench in 1947 he retired in 1968. He died aged 91 in 1993.

At Clerkenwell, in my early days, sat two men of very different stamp. These were Tom Davies and Frank Powell. Davies, both in dress and manner, belonged to a type of magistrate long gone. I never recall him wearing anything except the traditional wing collar and bow tie, black suit and striped trousers, together with a rose or carnation in his lapel. Yet although he was possessed of gravitas he also displayed, at times, a lively sense of humour. In a paternity case in which I appeared for the alleged father of the child, my client was an Indian of the name of Haque. "Hark hark the lark, eh Mr Bartle?" was Davies comment when I rose to my feet. On another occasion when I was in his court, defending counsel was appearing for a man charged with possession of pornographic photographs. Before the unfortunate advocate could develop the defence—such as it was—Davies exclaimed, "You don't need to tell me—its pure art!"

Frank Powell, although a colleague of Davies at Clerkenwell for many years was a man of very different character. He was a devout church man and active in Anglican circles. Powell was an understanding magistrate and always gave the defendant a fair hearing, but he had a disconcerting way of lying back in his chair with his eyes closed and his fingertips together. Sometimes I felt tempted to drop a book in order to discover whether he was attending to my argument or had in fact fallen asleep.

Mr Alan Stevenson, who sat at West London Court, possessed two claims to fame. The first was that he is the only stipendiary on record to have been shot at while on the bench. The bullet hole in the wall remains to this day. The second rests on the fact that he bore a quite remarkable resemblance to the former Prime Minister, Lord Home of the Hirschell. A colleague of mine once attended a dinner and, assuming that his neighbour was Stevenson, began discussing the crime lists at West London. His embarrassment was great when the Prime Minister was called upon to speak and "Alan Stevenson" rose.

My personal recollections cover eight chief magistrates. The first of these, before whom I occasionally appeared, was Sir Laurence Dunne. Dunne was a very patrician figure who, it is said, was not averse to wearing his Old Etonian tie on the bench. This would today be considered politically incorrect. In appearance, with his grey, immaculately groomed hair and moustache, he resembled a combination of a retired brigadier and a male film star of the 1930s vintage. He sat from time to time in the Chelsea domestic court where, in my first few years at the Bar, I sometimes did Poor Persons cases. The awe in which he was held was made apparent to me when I once disputed a point of matrimonial law with him. Afterwards the court usher muttered to me: "If you can stand up to Sir Laurence like that there is not much you can't do!" Yet personally I found him a benign and far from daunting tribunal.

Dunne's successor, Sir Robert Blundell, was a very formidable presence indeed. He looked every inch a Chief Metropolitan Magistrate. He was built like a rugby forward and was always very soberly dressed with a dark blue double-breasted pin-stripe suit, highly polished shoes, black, severely groomed hair and a somewhat immobile face. He exuded the gravitas of one who presided over London's magisterial law. He was not an easy tribunal before which to obtain an acquittal unless the prosecution had a very weak case indeed. I do not mean by this that he was biased.

Merely that his were not the sort of eyes over which the wool could easily be pulled. He had a somewhat disconcerting way of nodding agreement during counsel's closing address or speech in mitigation of sentence, only, at the conclusion of the case, to announce a decision which was quite the reverse of that for which the unfortunate advocate had been striving.

Sir Frank Milton, who followed Blundell was the chief magistrate at the time of my appointment to the metropolitan bench, and the first of those whom I came to know personally. I had been a member of the same leading criminal chambers in which he had enjoyed a substantial practice, and during my time there he encouraged me to apply for an appointment when he knew that I had ambitions in that direction. Milton was, in my view, intellectually head and shoulders above both his predecessors and those who followed. His manner, encapsulated in a balding dome and half-cut glasses, was that of a benevolent head-master, and the note of mild but firm authority was accentuated by the deep, carefully modulated voice. Milton was a most erudite man. He was the author of several books, the most important being *In Some Authority*, a history, albeit somewhat abbreviated, of the development of the metropolitan magistracy. A man of liberal outlook in a conservative tradition, he was scrupulously fair on the bench. He was the very last person who could have been accused of that old judicial vice of being biased in favour of the prosecution. However strong suspicion might be, if there was any doubt at the end of the day he unhesitatingly threw the case out. But most of all Milton stands out for the devotion which he gave to the body he represented. He was very firm in insisting that the professionalism of stipendiaries should be recognised and that only they should sit in court number one. He was instrumental in obtaining for the stipendiaries the right to sit as deputy circuit judges, and, if they should so require and proved suitable, as recorders and full judges in the Crown Court. His death, so early after retirement, was very sad.

After Milton came Sir Kenneth Barraclough. "Ken" Barraclough, as he was known to his contemporaries, was chief magistrate from 1975 to 1978. He was 68 on appointment. This was a more advanced age than would be the case today. At that time the retirement age for the stipendiary bench was 72, with the possibility of an extension to 75. Now the limit set at all levels of the judiciary is 70 and chief magistrates are not appointed over the age of 65. This is because of the very reasonable consideration that five full years of service is expected.

Sir Kenneth was educated at Oundle school and Clare College, Cambridge. Like many of his generation he had a military background having been in 1945 Colonel HQ, in the 21st Army Group, and was mentioned in dispatches. He was a member of the Inns of Court Regiment, and was honoured by the award of CBE and TD. Barraclough, although not an intellectual like Milton, was a solid, down-to-earth magistrate and is a very pleasant man to know on a personal level.

Between 1978 and 1982, the Chief Magistrate was Sir Evelyn Russell. It was during his time that I was invited to Bow Street where I have spent the remaining 20 years of my judicial service. Evelyn Russell was liked by all, and I can do no better than quote from his obituary notice in *The Times*:

> "Sir Evelyn Russell, the former Chief Metropolitan Magistrate, who has died aged 79, was respected for his courtesy and patience in court. If Russell was not given to making witty interjections or extravagant, headline-catching homilies he impressed all with whom he came into contact as a competent and exacting arbiter. After his appointment to the top magisterial post in England and Wales, however, Russell found it more difficult to keep out of the spotlight. Bow Street is the court where applications for extradition are made, and the more delicate cases with political dimensions usually come before the Chief Magistrate. A few months after he took up office Russell found himself presiding over the case of Astrid Proll, a fugitive terrorist sought by the West German government. Russell ruled that extradition was in order, in spite of Proll's plea of British citizenship following her marriage to an Englishman."

Evelyn was a devout Roman Catholic. He was awarded a papal knighthood, so it can be said that he was doubly honoured during his lifetime, once by church and once by state. He was a delightful man and I was very sad when he passed away.

From 1982 to 1992 the chief magistrate was Sir David Hopkin, a very different type of man from Russell, but one whom I came to know equally well. Hopkin, who died at the age of 75 uniquely combined the offices of Chief Metropolitan Stipendiary Magistrate and President of the British Boxing Board of Control. In both capacities he was a very distinctive figure.

David Armand Hopkin was educated at St Paul's school, West Kensington and University College, Aberystwyth, before going on to Corpus Christi College, Cambridge where he obtained a Bachelor of Arts degree.

After military service, in which he attained the rank of honorary major, he was called to the Bar by Gray's Inn. He entered the staff of the Director of Public Prosecutions on which he served for 20 years until his appointment as a metropolitan stipendiary magistrate in 1970.

Hopkin soon established his reputation on the bench as a firm, but compassionate magistrate and was always ready to inject his own brand of humour where this was appropriate. He did not find it easy to cope with verbose or tedious advocates but he manfully avoided interrupting as far as possible.

Off the bench, in private conversation, it was another matter. Hopkin could express himself in very forthright, and sometimes indecorous terms. Nevertheless, his positive approach to life and to his work undoubtedly contributed to his eventual selection as chief from among several other "hopefuls" in 1982. It was after this date that I got to know him personally since we had adjoining rooms at Bow Street Court.

The office of chief magistrate calls for administrative ability in addition to the judicial expertise which is expected of every stipendiary. This Hopkin undoubtedly possessed. As vice-chairman to his chairmanship of the Committee of Magistrates I came to respect the shrewd and decisive way in which he conducted the proceedings.

Every man has his critics and Hopkin was no exception to this universal rule. Some felt that his style was too confrontational and that he took criticism too personally. Yet he had some impressive qualities. One of his most likeable traits was his readiness to support a colleague who had come under criticism for one reason or another. Yet another was his complete lack of pomposity. Outside court hours we had many a long chat and his humour gave me a great deal of pleasure. David could sometimes speak in a very informal way. I recall one such occasion when a visitor to my court was the head of the Criminal Division of the Ministry of Justice in Tokyo. I thought I should introduce him to the chief magistrate. I knocked on David's door and ushered in my distinguished guest. David, thinking it was myself who was entering, said, "Come in, darling." The high-ranking member of the Japanese judicial system was surprised to be addressed in such endearing terms!

David Hopkin was Welsh to the core and he felt his roots in the principality very strongly. His father, Daniel Hopkin, had been a Liberal member of Parliament for a Welsh constituency and subsequently a stipendiary magistrate himself. David was also the type of person for whom work was the central feature of his life. He served as chief magistrate for a period of ten years, a substantially longer spell of duty in that office than a great many of his predecessors. But perhaps, for me, the most notable example of his devotion to duty was seen in the last two years of his service. At that time his health was failing badly and many a lesser man would have long since retired. With a rare courage he made light of this and continued to his final retirement date. He was a great family man. He met his charming wife, Doris, when they were undergraduates at Cambridge. They enjoyed a happy life-long marriage.

Sir Peter Badge followed David Hopkin. His years in office were from 1992 to 1997. His appointment marked a new departure since he was the first solicitor to receive this honour, although solicitors had been eligible for the appointment for some time. Peter, who kindly secured for me the post of deputy chief magistrate, became a firm friend of mine during his time at Bow Street. Our association was a very happy one. Peter Badge, who since his retirement sits as a recorder in the West Country, came to the chief magistracy at a time of great change and upheaval in the administration of justice, much of which impinged upon the Inner London magistrates' courts. His background as a senior partner in a substantial firm of solicitors and his membership of the Law Society Committee on Criminal Law; the Lord Chancellor's Advisory Committee for Inner London; the Magisterial Committee of the Judicial Studies Board and chairmanship of the Legal Committee of the Magistrates' Association were all very good experience to enable him to cope with the flood of new administrative proposals and plans with which the magistrates' courts were being inundated at this time. These developments had their effect on the chief magistrate's office in that it increasingly became an administrative and less of a judicial task. I was pleased to be able to take some of the pressure off Peter Badge by sitting in some of the more time-consuming cases involving extradition applications and lengthy submissions by defence advocates.

Finally there came the present chief, the charming and personable Graham Edward Parkinson. Also a solicitor, Graham, like his predecessors, is the incumbent at a time of great change for the stipendiary bench. That anticipated change, in terms of title and national structure, is destined to take place during his time and he will doubtless handle these matters with the great competence he has already displayed during his first years of office.

To know someone is not necessarily to love them, but as I come up to my retirement I have a great sense of gratitude at having been privileged to spend my career among colleagues who have been good people to know and work with. It is cause for regret that while the quality of the stipendiary magistrates has improved, their status has declined. There is no justification for the greatly increased disparity of salary between the circuit and stipendiary bench. The absurd image of the stipendiary as dealing with drunks and trivial offenders still lingers on, notwithstanding the fact that a great deal of serious crime is dealt with in the metropolitan courts and that stipendiaries have the responsibility of sentence and judicial decision. At long last, and after many unfulfilled promises of rectification, the position is now being put right. The judicial expertise of the stipendiaries today is every bit as good as that of the circuit judges and should be recognised as such. Under the present administration I believe it will be.

CHAPTER 9

A Day in the Life of a London Magistrate

I was naturally proud to have been appointed to Bow Street Court since Bow Street and Great Marlborough Street, the latter now sadly closed, are the only two metropolitan courts to which a stipendiary appointment can only be made with the personal approval of the Lord Chancellor. This was a transition from East to West. It is an interesting fact that although each London court does similar work, there is a subtle difference of atmosphere, sentencing policy and predominant class of crime from one to another.

The first thing which struck me about Bow Street was the pace of the work compared with Thames. One had to get through one's cases at a brisk rate to finish the invariably heavy morning list by lunchtime. A whole range of decisions had to be made very quickly. The legendary drunks, prostitutes and street traders to which I have already referred, occupied a fraction of the whole. The entire panorama of West End crime presented itself in all its ugliness, absurdity and, sometimes, comedy. There is no other branch of the judiciary in which rulings have to be given so rapidly on every conceivable issue from the utterly trivial on the one hand to the immensely serious on the other. One example of this is the question of bail. Bail or custody is a question which arises very frequently when one of the remands, of which there are a great many, takes place. This may involve a petty thief with a record of minor dishonesty or an international fraudsman charged with the criminal appropriation of millions. The three choices are to grant bail, to grant it on conditions or to refuse bail altogether. In the case of the fraudsman there may be substantial sureties available, and yet his opportunities for absconding may remain high. The magistrate is invariably reminded that under the Bail Act 1976 there is a presumption in favour of bail and that the grounds on which it can be refused are effectively limited to the likelihood of the defendant absconding, the fear of the commission of further offences and interference with the course of justice. Coping with these, and other difficult decisions, caused me to think more deeply about my function and calling as a magistrate, and as to what extent I possessed the right qualities for my job. What were those qualities?

First, I must have a sound judicial sense. The whole duty of a magistrate is to administer justice—that subtle combination of judgment and mercy. There are so many virtues which go into the making of judicial character that it is difficult to enumerate them. Sir John Fielding, an early Bow Street magistrate, was described on his death as having been "a consummate magistrate who was universally allowed to have the head of a philosopher, the heart of a Christian and the hand of a hero."

A member of the bench who lacks judicial qualities, and occasionally it does occur, can be a disaster. There are few occupations in which a "misfit" can do so much damage, and nowhere is the maladministration of justice more glaringly exposed than in the magistrates' court. The story has been told, hopefully apocryphal of a magistrates' court in which a particular local solicitor was frequently instructed to defend the area's miscreants. One morning his familiar figure was seen in court and he rose before the bench to announce that in the case being called on he represented the prosecution. The chairman peered over his spectacles and proclaimed, "Nice to have you on our side for a change." An equally unlikely tale is that of the chairman who told the defendant at the conclusion of a case, "We think that there may be a doubt, but you are not having the benefit of it."

Judicial sense is the gift of being able to separate personal feelings and promptings from a cool and impartial appraisal of the case. It means one must never reach a conclusion until all the evidence has been heard. It compels total adherence to the principle that if there is a lurking doubt the defendant must be acquitted, whatever one's private reactions to him or her may be. Above all, it calls for a total absence of prejudice of any kind.

Another essential attribute of a good magistrate is humility. The prophet Isiah states, "I dwell in the high and holy place, with him also that is of a contrite and humble spirit, to revive the spirit of the humble, and to revive the heart of the contrite one." It is sometimes said that justices of the peace are pillars of society, but few modern magistrates would welcome that description. There seems to be something pharisaical in the idea of a moral ornament, laying down precepts and standards for the rest of mankind. On the other hand they are not social reformers. While seeking to adopt a constructive approach, they sometimes have to apply the retributive factor irrespective of whether or not it helps to reform the offender.

The third essential attribute of a magistrate is knowledge. "A wise man is strong; yea a man of knowledge increaseth strength" says the Book of Proverbs, and the words hold much truth on the bench. Gone are the days when a magistrate could expect to rely entirely upon the court clerk for advice on all matters of law and evidence. Of course such advice is extremely useful and should be sought in moments of difficulty. A well-known magistrate of years ago was once asked how he disposed of his cases with such remarkable speed. He replied "My clerk listens without deciding while I decide without listening." This would not be an example to follow. Even a lay magistrate today is expected to have a working knowledge of the criminal law, the basic precepts of evidence and the sentencing powers available to the court.

One of the first things I discovered at Bow Street was the excellence of the court clerks. For most of my time the chief clerk was Mrs Ferley, or Joyce as she was known to us all. Joyce Ferley not only managed the administrative side of the court with great efficiency, but possessed an almost encyclopaedic knowledge of magisterial law and procedure, together with a very special expertise in the field of extradition. Without exception all the deputies were very good at their job. Stipendiary magistrates have the advantage over circuit judges in this respect. In the Crown Court the clerk has certain procedural duties to carry out, but the judge cannot rely upon him or her for the kind of advice which is available to a stipendiary.

The relationship between a magistrate and his or her clerk is a very special, almost personal one. It is quite different from that of a judge and the clerk in a Crown Court. In the Crown Court the judge effectively "runs" the proceedings in addition to fulfilling his judicial duties. The role of the clerk, as I have indicated, is more formal in nature. Magistrates and their clerks, however, work in "harness" and a fine balance must be maintained to ensure that the one does not usurp or encroach upon the functions of the other. If this is true of a lay bench how much more does it apply to a metropolitan court with a stipendiary magistrate sitting alone. The stipendiary and his or her clerk can be compared to pilot and navigator, or perhaps actor and prompter. The one has the ultimate responsibility for decision making; the other must attend to the conduct of the proceedings and correct the magistrate if he or she should err on matters of law or procedure. The personality factor is inescapable. Dr Johnson said, "No two men can be half an hour together but one shall acquire an evident superiority over the other." A strong clerk can exercise a disproportionate influence over a pliable magistrate, while an unduly self-assertive magistrate may humiliate a deferential clerk. I recall a senior chief clerk whose method of making newly appointed stipendiaries aware of their limitations was to correct their inaccuracies in a loud voice audible throughout the court after the error had occurred. On the other hand I knew of a chairman of the bench whose reaction to being corrected by his clerk was something close to indignation.

The essence of a good relationship between magistrate and clerk consists first, in correct observance of the demarcation of duties and, secondly, an atmosphere of mutual respect and regard in the performance of those duties. These principles are sometimes more easily stated than put into effect. *Stone's Justices' Manual,* describes the position as follows:

> "The functions of a justices' clerk include the giving to the justices to whom he is clerk or any of them, at the request of the justices or justice, of advice about law, practice or procedure on questions arising in connection with the discharge of their or his functions including questions arising when the clerk is not personally attending on the justices or justice; the clerk may at any time when he thinks he should do so bring to the attention of the justices or justice any point of law, practice or procedure that is or may be involved in any questions so arising."

A Day in the Life of a London Magistrate

This is quite a "mouthful," but it encapsulates the enormous help which I have received in performing my duties from the court clerks, particularly those at Bow Street.

> "The 1981 *Practice Direction* sets out in more detail the role of the clerk in court: 'First, the clerk must be prepared to advise the bench out of court on questions of law, mixed fact and law, practice and procedure. Secondly, he or she is liable, if called upon, to refresh the justice's memory as to any matters of evidence and to draw attention to any issues involved in the matters before the court. Thirdly the clerk must be ready to advise the court on the range of penalties which the law allows it to impose and the principle of law attaching to those penalties.'"

There is clearly a completely different affinity between a stipendiary and his or her clerk to that of the clerk with a lay bench. Stipendiaries, being qualified lawyers, are presumed to know the law and also to be acquainted with the rules of evidence. In theory they should not need to be advised on these matters. Nevertheless, professional magistrates are just as prone to the occasional error as their lay brethren and the clerk's responsibility applies in the same way. It may take considerable courage on the part of a very junior clerk to offer unsolicited correction to the senior stipendiary magistrate, but if the occasion requires it, this must be done without hesitation. I personally always welcome correction. Perhaps this is because of the frequency with which I need it! By the same token a young magistrate should reject advice which he or she considers unsound, albeit from a normally reliable source.

What is quite insupportable, but happily I have never experienced, is an open disagreement in court between the bench and its clerk. To avoid this can call for diplomacy of the highest order on both sides. A harmonious relationship is vital to the ordered administration of justice. I have always liked my clerk to speak in a loud, clear and authoritative voice. One of the problems for lady clerks, of whom there are many more today than formerly, is that some of them have very quiet voices. This is not easily corrected since a person's voice is very much a part of their personality. One cannot tell a mild-mannered young woman to start speaking like a sergeant major. But it does create an obstacle between the court and the defendant if the latter, many of whom are from ethnic minorities, cannot hear or understand what is being said to them.

It is a moot point as to what extent the clerk should "run" the court. The *Practice Direction* says:

> "The clerk may conduct the ordinary arrangements inside the court, assist it as to the relevance of evidence, ask questions of witnesses to clear up ambiguities; but there is no general or accepted practice, and essentially the conduct of the proceedings is a matter for agreement between the justices, and the clerk."

The crucial words here are "a matter for agreement." I personally have always adopted the policy of not interfering in the control and conduct of the proceedings except, when necessary, to support the clerk if "back up" authority is called for. Matters which are entirely within the province of the clerk are calling on cases, taking the plea and election, informing a defendant of his or her options at the close of the prosecution case, controlling order in court, assisting unrepresented defendants, directing the usher in his or her duties and correcting witnesses as necessary. A delicate situation can arise when there is a possibility of a case being resolved with a bind-over. A judicious inquiry by the clerk, supported by appropriate exhortations from the bench is generally an effective synchronism, to secure a shortening of the proceedings.

A difficult problem is when, if ever, the clerk should correct counsel. Advocates in general feel themselves to be answerable to the magistrate and not to the clerk. What should the clerk do when the advocate misquotes or omits to refer accurately to the law, asks patently leading questions or seeks to induce inadmissible evidence? The answer is that the clerk has a duty to intervene, but the interjection should be by way of advice to the magistrate rather than chastisement of the advocate.

Should the clerk ever advise on the correct sentence in any particular case? The answer must be a clear negative. However, the clerk may perfectly properly give advice to the court which influences and even changes the magistrate's mind. Thus he may advise that technical difficulties stand in the way of one form of sentence so causing the court to dispose of the case differently. On questions of bail also the clerk, in eliciting reasons from the police for their opposition, may influence the view of the bench.

Should a magistrate and his clerk discuss, after the court has risen, the sentences passed or the verdicts reached? I believe very strongly that they should not. Such a conversation places the clerk in the embarrassing position of having to support the actions of the magistrate even though he may think otherwise, or give expression to his disagreement thus causing anxiety and concern.

These are some of the principles to which I have tried to adhere in my relationship with the clerks at Bow Street. Without exception I received wonderful service from them, men and women, senior and deputies, legally qualified and not so qualified. I can see no justification for the policy recently announced of insisting that all court clerks should be qualified solicitors or members of the Bar. Many of those who are promoted from office work to court functions are perfectly competent to discharge their new duties, and in any event are paid on a substantially lower salary scale than those with qualifications.

Now let me turn to relationships with the advocates who have appeared before me during my 20 years at Bow Street. First of all the prosecutors. Until 1987 when the Crown Prosecution Service was launched, much of the prosecuting in minor cases was conducted by the police themselves. I have never doubted that this was a highly unsatisfactory state of affairs. The police are not suited either by training or temperament for the business of advocacy. There was something undesirable about police officers prosecuting in their own cause. Their interest in obtaining a conviction was too personal. A burly police sergeant might well be an excellent officer, but he was at an obvious disadvantage if placed in opposition to a skilful defending lawyer. Even when the prosecution were represented by a trained advocate, the practice of calling the police as witnesses to deal with antecedent history, even in trivial cases, involved a great waste of police time. I recall the serried ranks of policemen sitting all morning in court waiting for their cases to be called when they could and should have been better employed carrying out their proper duties, namely policing. On other issues, such as bail, it was normal procedure to call the officer into the witness box to give objections and be cross-examined—thus consuming a great deal of court time. Yet this is how things were for my first nine years at Bow Street.

It is strange how unpopular new ideas can be even before they have been tried out. Some powerful arguments were advanced against the whole concept of the CPS. A full-time salaried government-employed court prosecutor is a novel concept in this country. The English Bar has always prided itself upon its independence. To prosecute one day and defend the next is quite common for a criminal barrister and is equally proper and permissible for a solicitor advocate. The popular idea that there is a cynical aspect to this is misconceived. There might, in fact, be said to be something healthy in the concept of an advocate who is not always striving for convictions or acquittals, but sees his role in a more detached light as merely providing a competent service for whichever side engages him.

It is strange to realise that a similarly hostile attitude was once adopted towards the concept of professional policemen and stipendiary magistrates. The traditional mistrust of the state-employed official has a long history in this country. Is it desirable to have a nationwide body of professional men and women whose careers and promotion prospects depend to some, if not to a large extent, on their achieving successful results in criminal prosecutions, it was asked. Another major question was whether sufficient advocates could be found to take over the immense amount of prosecuting work in the country at large, quite apart from in the metropolis. This was to some extent met by the employment of agents, but the modesty of the fees which were offered was not such as to guarantee a sizeable response. Yet another cause for concern was the cost of employing such a large body of prosecutors on a regular basis. Nobody seriously supposed that the amount recovered in costs would be sufficient to make the new service entirely self-financing.

Notwithstanding these concerns I was one of those who was strongly favourable to the institution of the CPS. I always believed that once the "teething" troubles had been overcome the result would be to speed up and streamline the process of justice. I considered that the new system, and those whose task it was to make it work, should be given a chance and that it was churlish to criticise too hastily and too readily. Some of my colleagues did not seem to share my view.

By and large I have been impressed with our CPS prosecutors at Bow Street, although I appreciate that this has not been the experience of my colleagues in some of the other courts. The young men and women prosecutors are under immense pressure. They have to work their way through lists which may consist of 30 or more cases. Notwithstanding the fact that many of these are trivial in character, in each one the facts must be outlined and antecedents dealt with. The Crown prosecutor has to be well-informed regarding objections to bail, and not infrequently has an uphill and embarrassing task when applying for an adjournment which may be necessary due to an administrative error on the part of the police or CPS. It is a task which requires great alertness of mind, concentration and industry. Because one advocate is handling the whole list, when things do go amiss more disruption occurs than under the old system. But the advantages of the new system over the old are very apparent. Court business is undoubtedly dispatched at a greater speed than before. The police are released for more important duties and their court functions have been taken over by those whose training fits them for the work.

Sometimes adjournments are requested due to a breakdown in communication between the CPS and the police. Most of the adjournments of cases, I find, are because of recently built-in procedures such as the provision of advance information to the defence.

One thing which has caused me concern in my experience with the CPS is the tendency to bring summary only charges, perhaps on the basis of an anticipated plea of guilty, or because a conviction is thought easier to obtain before a stipendiary magistrate than before a jury. On one such occasion the defendant was charged with a number of offences of using his private computer to place items of child pornography on to the internet. He was asking for over 100 other offences to be taken into consideration. The maximum penalty I was able to pass was six months' imprisonment. This I did, but I was dismayed at the limitation upon my sentencing powers. I have also been occasionally surprised when a case is discontinued. But in this latter situation I do not think it appropriate for the bench to question the exercise of their discretion by the CPS.

Is the CPS to be welcomed? I think it is. Now that many of the initial difficulties have been overcome the greater speed and professionalism of the new system as against the old will fully justify its arrival. One thing is certain, the CPS is here to stay and when that situation prevails the only sensible course is to make it work well.

I now turn to the defence advocates. One of the principal impressions I have received at Bow Street has been the high standard of advocacy on the part of the local solicitors who appear before me on a regular basis. Many of these belong to our duty solicitor scheme. The legal aid arrangements which exist today in both Crown Courts and magistrates' courts is infinitely superior to the situation which prevailed during my early days at the Bar in the mid-50s. This is something which should be borne in mind when the question of cost is debated.

When I started at the Bar there were, broadly speaking, two methods by which unrepresented poor defendants could obtain counsel. One was by means of the dock brief and the other was assignment in court. These operated in what in those days were Quarter Sessions and Assizes. The dock brief, which was brilliantly portrayed in John Mortimer's first West End success, was an extraordinarily antiquated procedure. Young, and sometimes not so young, members of the Bar sat in counsel's row while the defendant was brought round to the front and instructed to select from among their number the one who he would like to defend him. It would have been an interesting subject for research as to the reasons behind the choices which were made. If this were on the basis of the most intelligent looking it would seem to have escaped the notice of the prisoner that the brightest members of the English Bar were not generally to be found in search of a dock brief. Seniority was somewhat obscured by the presence of the wig. This traditional mode of legal disguise could sometimes also confuse the issue of sex. A less than glamorous lady was once chosen with the words, "I will have that gentleman there." After the defendant had exercised his preference an even less dignified process followed.

The lucky counsel descended to the cell to give their newly acquired client the unwelcome news that he must part with the sum of two pounds and two shillings in order to acquire a "mouthpiece." For an advocate to take less than the traditional sum would have been professionally improper. The embarrassment to counsel was sometimes exacerbated by members of the family rummaging in their pockets and handbags to make good any shortfall there might have been. Clients acquired in this manner were not, in my experience, particularly sensitive about the ethics of the Bar. Having parted with a good coin of the realm they took the view that whatever they may have done it was the job of a barrister to tell the court that they had not done it. It came as a rude shock to be told that if they admitted the crime there must be a plea of guilty and that the most their counsel could do was to mitigate sentence. On the other hand if one's client insisted on his or her innocence their story, however unlikely, had to be presented to the jury in the best possible light. The fact that this whole absurd procedure survived for so long is a comment upon the English reverence for tradition.

The other method by which fledgling barristers were instructed on behalf of indigent defendants was on appointment by the court clerk. It was in this way that I received my first brief. A barrister's first brief is a landmark in his or her life and I have before me the papers in the case. At the time I received it I had gone along to the Old Bailey to merely "sit in" and acquire experience as a newly called member of the Bar. Nothing was further from my mind than the prospect of actually representing somebody. But my equanimity was short-lived when I was handed a court brief by the clerk to mitigate on behalf of a man who had pleaded guilty to several charges of theft as a servant. The defendant was an import manager for a firm of wholesalers in the paper industry. In a sentence, he had been privately disposing of property imported to his company from the continent. The sums involved were quite modest by today's standards, but the fact that he had abused a position of trust made the matter more serious than might otherwise have been the case. For the first time I learned about the human tragedy of crime and the terrible suffering it inflicts upon all who are its victims.

The defendant was a middle-aged man of hitherto good character who blamed his folly on involvement with drink, gambling and living beyond his means. He was married with two children and was purchasing their home through a building society. He had had an excellent record of service in the Army. I notice on re-reading the papers someone had written on one of the pages as if in anticipation of the sentence "Probation?" He received four years' imprisonment. I have often wondered what became of his marriage, his children and his home. I have discovered that to be preoccupied about such matters would render the job of an advocate or a judge impossible.

My experience of advocates at Bow Street has been very mixed. Most of our local solicitors are competent and courteous. They make their points neatly and with commendable brevity—bearing in mind the value of time when the court is working its way through a heavy list. But a few of the advocates I hear, in which I include some younger members of the Bar, would clearly be wise to seek some other form of employment. A great deal of advocacy in magistrates' courts is mitigation. I have always thought that it is better to make no point at all than to make a bad point. This is frustrating to listen to because although I have been on the bench for 27 years, mitigation still makes a substantial difference to my decision. It can make the difference between a man or woman going to prison or retaining their liberty.

Throughout my career in the law I have periodically lectured to students on advocacy and I have always tried to emphasise the futility of bad argument. What is the significance of a defendant being sorry—who isn't sorry after being caught? If goods have been recovered after a theft there is little credit in this for an accused person if he or she was relieved of them only after a chase. I have always made it a golden rule not to interrupt, but there are times when this is well-nigh impossible. I have always emphasised to aspiring members of the Bar when lecturing at the Inns of Court School of Law or at the weekend conference centre Cumberland Lodge, that there are five considerations for an advocate. These are appearance, manner, presentation, content and duration.

I acquired a somewhat "fuddy-duddy" reputation for maintaining the virtues of sobriety in dress for court advocates in magistrates' courts. The

A Day in the Life of a London Magistrate

"uniform" of wig and gown is not worn at this judicial level. White shirts and dark ties are preferable to colourful shirts and startling ties. Manner is important because it sets the tone of the proceedings. An advocate should have a pleasant and respectful manner. To be nice to those from whom one seeks something in return is not hypocrisy, it is plain common sense. Pomposity of any kind, particularly in the young, is extremely unattractive. This is also true of those who address the court with their hands in their pockets or one foot on the bench beside them. To be seen reading a newspaper or a novel in court indicates a lack of interest in the proceedings generally. I have noticed, in recent years, a tendency towards lack of good court manners. An advocate who is out of court when the case is called on should always apologise for not being present. He may be blameless but contrition is politic. The advocate's pride should be sacrificed in the client's interest. There is also an increasing practice of taking instructions in the dock without first obtaining the leave of the court to do so.

One of the most regrettable things I encounter as a magistrate is poor presentation. I am sorry to say this but there are some advocates who would benefit from a course of instruction in elocution. An advocate who speaks too softly or too quickly will irritate the bench. It must be remembered that in later life most people do not enjoy such acute hearing as they did in their younger days. A loud clear voice and good diction are a pleasure in court.

The most difficult part of advocacy is, by common consent, cross-examination. It is unrealistic to expect a young prosecutor or defender to have fully mastered this art. Yet it has to be said that it is extremely rare to hear good cross-examination from either the prosecution or defence in my court at Bow Street. Mere confrontation with phrases such as, "I suggest," or "I put it to you," achieve precisely nothing. Many is the time I have felt tempted to give a helping hand—but it is a temptation I have to resist.

I have always had a very conservative, some would say old-fashioned, attitude about the use of the English language. This has brought criticism, but I have not changed my views. I wince when I hear reference to kids instead of children, pub rather than public house, mum and dad in place of mother and father. I have heard this sort of language in court:

> "These two police see a punch-up going on. They charge into the scene and grab this gentleman (indicating the defendant). He breaks free and scarpers, but he gets picked up two hours later hanging about in a pub."

I have heard mitigation like this:

> "I am going to ask the court to treat this as very much a one-off affair. It is true that a few years ago he had several offences on the trot, but the trouble was alcohol and he has been on the wagon for the last three years."

Abbreviation has become so common that is seems almost churlish to correct it. ABH, GBH and TDA have replaced actual bodily harm, grievous bodily harm and taking and driving away. The drift away from good, acceptable and accurate English in the courts is dangerous. We have given our great and unique language to the world. Surely we ourselves have a special duty to maintain it, pure and unsullied.

I would like to say now a brief word about the probation service and to pay my tribute to a body of men and women who give such devoted service to the administrators of justice. There was a time, in my experience, when a younger breed of probation officers, like their social worker counterparts, had an approach to their work which had ideological overtones. Some of them were opposed to the idea of imprisonment in virtually any circumstances. Consequently their reports to the court were not always helpful.

I have never found this to be the case at Bow Street where we enjoy the services of probation officers of maturity and experience. I have always relied heavily on their wisdom and advice. I find the pre-sentence report a much more helpful document than the old reports which could be requested for any kind of offence, and tended to be a "fall back" when the court could not think of what should be done. The pre-sentence report helps greatly in cases where custody is a strong likelihood but a community sentence may suffice.

Perhaps, last of all, I should speak about defendants. As a magistrate one develops a certain rapport with those confronting one from the dock. It is rare that I feel any animosity, save in exceptionally nasty cases. One rule I have always observed is to give my reasons both for sentence and for a guilty verdict. There is a traditional viewpoint that magistrates are not obliged to give reasons.[1] This is a principle with which I have never been able to agree. When people are sentenced they are entitled to know why a particular disposal has been chosen. Equally it is proper that they should be told why the court has decided the case against them.

---

1. As noted earlier there is nowadays a statutory duty to give reasons in many situations.

CHAPTER 10

A Little of Myself

I was born into a clerical family. My father was a clergyman as also was his brother. One of my cousins went into the ministry and became a canon. Yet notwithstanding this strong tradition my own calling was ultimately to the law, not the church.

I do not find genealogy a particularly absorbing subject. If there is a prospect of turning up something particularly interesting I am sure that the expenditure of time and money on the necessary research is well justified. If this is not the case I have my doubts as to the usefulness of the exercise.

The most interesting forebear of whom I am aware is my paternal great grandfather. The Reverend George Bartle DD, LLD, known in the family as Grandfather Bartle. He was educated at the then famous University of Jena in Prussia where he received doctorates in law and divinity. He was headmaster of a school in Southport, Lancashire, and was also a prolific author. Some his books were of a religious, others of an educational character. The former works, heavily Protestant in tone, included such titles as *The Scriptural Doctrine of Hades, An Analysis and Exposition of the Church Catechism, Dissertation on the Sacrifice of Christ.* The educational works numbered among them *Epitome of English Grammar* and *A Synopsis of English History.* This last, of which I have a copy, was published in 1876. The ambitious nature of the undertaking may be illustrated by the introductory description:

> "A concise yet full account of the wars, leading events, and persons of note in each reign; together with genealogical charts, chronological tables, terms of the various treaties, contemporary sovereigns, British colonies, historic rhymes, and explanatory remarks."

This book enjoyed a considerable degree of success in the educational field and ran into three editions. I have little further information regarding my great grandfather, but his labours as a clergyman, a teacher and an author would suggest he fully embraced the Victorian work ethic.

My paternal grandfather was one of three sons. He was employed with a firm of London solicitors. He had two sons and a daughter, one of the two sons being my father. My father, also the Reverend George Bartle, after a curacy in Surrey, became Vicar of Christ Church, Spitalfields, a few years before the outbreak of the Second World War. As a very small boy I was entered for the City of London School, but since my efforts in the mathematics paper consisted of my name, the number one and a smudge, my presence at that particular school was no longer required. Perhaps I should have studied my great grandfather's book *Vulgar Fractions Made Easy*. Consequently I was sent to a private boarding school in Redhill which was run by two maiden ladies of a type not uncommon in those days. George Orwell has delivered himself of some very unflattering sentiments regarding private boarding schools of the 1930s, but on the basis of my own recollections, his comments are not unjustified. Private schools of that era fulfilled a need for middle-class parents who, while on the one hand being unable to afford expensive preparatory and public schools for their children, were equally unwilling to send them to the elementary working-class schools which was all the state had to offer at that time. Such schools were frequently housed in private buildings which had been converted into a place of education and which were often wholly inappropriate accommodation for this purpose. Operated, as they often were, on a financial shoestring the food was abysmal, even by the general standards of the time, and the teachers poorly qualified. My sojourn at this particular institution was interrupted by the outbreak of war—an event which for me personally brought a merciful release.

Spitalfields Church, which presides elegantly over an area of London rich in history, is a masterpiece of ecclesiastical architecture designed by Nicholas Hawksmoor and built between 1714 and 1729. The region was already fairly well developed when the Revocation of the Edict of Nantes, and the massacre of St Bartholomew's night which followed, sent a flood of Huguenot refugees across the Channel to swell the already existing community of silk weavers in the parish. The trade, however, was a precarious one, and although some of the fine houses in the streets around the church reflect the prosperity of the richer weavers, many were less fortunate. The development of mechanical looms spelt the end of the road for the hand-weavers and very few survived the changes. At the turn of the 19th century a new wave of immigrants arrived. These were Eastern European Jews, also fleeing from persecution in their native lands. Unlike the Huguenots, whose trade had virtually disappeared, the Jews were tailors and furriers and many prospered sufficiently by their industriousness to progress to more salubrious parts of London.

Finally, in the post-Second World War period, came the new arrivals from Bangladesh. These too brought their entrepreneurial skills to the district and at the present time they are the dominant foreign element. They have not, however, been absorbed by the host country to anything like the degree of the two earlier groups. A building at the opposite end of Fournier Street from Christ Church symbolises the history of immigration to the region. It began as a Huguenot chapel. Later it became a synagogue and today is a mosque.

The heroic days of the East End were, of course, the legendary period of the "Blitz." Hitler, infuriated that, contrary to his assurances to the German people, Berlin had been bombed, gave the order for the large scale bombing of London, in particular the docklands. Churchill's imperishable words prepared London for the ordeal:

> "Here, in this great city of refuge, wherein are enshrined the title deeds of human progress, we await, undismayed, the impending assault."

That assault, when it came, very much included Spitalfields in the centre of which was my father's church and rectory. He organized an air raid shelter in the crypt of his church which, like many of the makeshift shelters in London probably provided psychological rather than very secure physical protection. But for the hundreds who spent night after night there as the bombs rained down the accommodation, though uncomfortable, was welcome. There were some ancient stone coffins in the crypt, allegedly of Roman origin. One individual slept regularly in one of these. No doubt he felt that the stone surround would provide protection against blast, and in any event, should anything unfortunate happen, he was conveniently placed.

After the high-explosive bombs there came the incendiaries which ignited fires across London. I remember as a boy the excitement of finding the burnt-out remains of some of these. December 29, 1940 was the night of the second Great Fire of London, immortalised in the famous photograph of St Paul's Cathedral outlined against the background of a burning city. Several incendiaries fell on the roof of Christ Church, and my father, who climbed up to the roof with the firefighters, looked out over what he described as "a sea of flames in all directions." The life of an East End vicar was busy in those days — helping the emergency services, organizing shelter and refreshment for the people of the locality, comforting the injured and praying with the dying. Sadly, my father never kept a diary.

I was a boy of ten years when the war broke out. I was at morning service in a country church with my mother and sister. A note was passed to the priest conducting the service and he announced that this country was at war with Germany. I recall a sense of real fear which I never experienced again — even when I was actually blown over by the blast from a flying bomb during my schooldays in 1943. Those schooldays were spent at St John's, Leatherhead, a minor but well-regarded public (or should I now say independent) school, noted for its large intake of sons of the clergy. Whether or not this is an indication of moral excellence is debatable, but having survived the traditionally miserable early period as a non-person I found life there not uncongenial. Fortunately I excelled at sport — always a factor in one's favour at an English boarding school.

After school came National Service. The fairly tough life of a public school had been good preparation both physically and psychologically for the rigours of primary and infantry training. Yet I never had the makings of a soldier. On one occasion I was placed under close arrest for having forgotten to clean the rust off my bayonet. I was marched to the guardroom, where my presence went so unremarked that when, after what I considered to be an appropriate period, I wandered off, nobody sought to detain me. I became a sergeant-instructor in the Royal Army

Education Corps. The lecturing and debating I engaged in first fired me with a desire to go to the Bar. I also took part in boxing and was a reserve member of the Army athletic team—activities which enabled me to justify to myself membership of an honourable corps for which some of the more "macho" regiments held a less than flattering opinion.

In 1948 I was posted to Detmold in the military district of Hanover. I had seen bomb damage in London, but the sight which met my eyes when our train entered Hanover Station was one which I shall never forget. The destruction was as near total as I had ever seen. For as far as the eye could see there was nothing but brick rubble and the shattered remains of buildings. Yet I was told that Hamburg and Cologne were worse! I was stationed with the First Royal Tank Regiment, colloquially known as the Desert Rats. The regiment subsequently won further honours in the Gulf War.

Cambridge followed the Army and the magic of that ancient university is with me still. The beauty of the colleges has always made a deep impression on me, particularly my own college, Jesus. The architecture is a perfect blend of the medieval, 17th century, early-Victorian and modern, and the lawns and flowerbeds are delightfully laid out. After reading history for two years I switched to law. I was privileged to have as my tutor Professor, now Sir, Robert Jennings, who later became president of the International Court. Those were the days when the great Professor Lauterpacht lectured in international law. I attended many of his lectures, delivered as they were with a dry humour. I have to admit, however, that the social life of the university absorbed a great deal of my attention during term time and most of my academic work was done in the vacation. It was during my time that Julien Slade wrote his great musical success *Salad Days*. One lyric I especially recall:

> "Wherever we go, whatever we do the magic will hold us still. Sometimes we may pretend to forget, but of course we never will. We mustn't say these were our happiest days, whatever our memories are. We mustn't say these were our happiest days—but our happiest days so far. And if I start looking behind me, and want to retrace my track, remember to remind me, we said we'd never look back."

I have never tried to retrace my track, but I haven't forgotten—and never will.

After Cambridge came Lincoln's Inn. I was called to the Bar in February 1954 by the then treasurer Lord Cohen. At that time the great majority of Bar students were from the Commonwealth. Only about five of us were English. One of these was a certain Margaret Roberts, now known to a wider public as Lady Thatcher. I still retain the dinner menu of that night with her signature upon it. Perhaps some day it may be of interest to Christie's or Sotheby's.

The experience of becoming a member of Lincoln's Inn was akin to that of first starting at Cambridge. Indeed there are several notable similarities between an Inn of Court and an Oxbridge college. The ancient Dining Hall, The Chapel, The Library, the lovely grounds and gardens and the collegiate atmosphere with its ancient historical tradition—all these are factors in common. Even the residential aspect was once part of life in the Inns, though in the distant past. Lincoln's Inn is undoubtedly the most beautiful of the four Inns of Court. The Inner Temple was virtually demolished during the "Blitz" and was little more than a pile of rubble when I began in chambers as a pupil. The Middle Temple was virtually spared although the beautiful carved wooden screen in the Dining Hall was blown to pieces, and subsequently reconstructed by a piece of almost miraculously skilled craftsmanship. Gray's Inn has always seemed to me to be the "odd man out" among the Inns of Court. But I have no doubt that those who were called there hold it in high esteem.

There is a well worn saying about the Bar—"many are called but few are chosen." This adage was particularly applicable in the immediate post-war years. To say that there was very little work for beginners would be an understatement. There was virtually none. And this in a profession in which the early years are invariably lean. I had read how the great advocate Sir Patrick Hastings, in his early years, inserted cardboard into his shoes because he was unable to afford a new pair. I was never reduced to such a stratagem. Had this happened it would have been the only point of comparison between myself and Hastings. I was obliged, however, to find some way of acquiring a minimum income while surviving at the Bar in those early days. This I managed to do by the well-tried expedient of giving evening lectures and marking correspondence college papers. In this way, in common with others in my situation, I managed to keep body and soul together. I enjoyed the added advantage of being able to live at home during those years. It was fortunate that my dear mother did not require payment for my keep. None, I fear, was forthcoming.

I served two separate pupillages, one civil and one criminal. I was not sure at that time which branch of the law I intended to enter. Indeed, I would have been grateful for an opening in any branch at all. My first pupil master was Neil Mackinon, QC, later to be an Old Bailey judge. He was a helpful and pleasant pupil master, but I soon realised that civil work, with its pleadings, statements of claim, interrogatories etc., was not for me. My second pupillage was in the chambers of Mr John Huxley Buzzard. Buzzard's practice consisted entirely of criminal prosecutions, and since he was a Treasury counsel these consisted mostly of heavy fraud trials. I benefited very little from my time with him. The work was far over my head as a fledgling barrister, and he was not an understanding or helpful pupil master. He did not suffer fools gladly, and I, so far as he was concerned, fell very much into that category.

Pupillage over, I entered the Chambers of Mr Neil Taylor, QC, at 2 Dr Johnson's Buildings. A few of the senior members had acquired practices but for newcomers there was virtually no work at all. It was during this period of my life that I made a brief, though unsuccessful, foray into politics. At Cambridge I had been treasurer of the University Conservative Association but I never seriously contemplated a political career. I did not see myself as in any sense a "political animal." I am not the hard-driving extrovert type who excels in that particular sphere of activity. However, one commodity which I had in abundance as a young barrister was spare time, and when the opportunity to contest a Parliamentary seat came my way I had no hesitation in taking it. The constituency in question was Islington North. At no time did I suffer from the illusion that I might win the seat. It was, and remains, impregnably Labour. That responsibility removed I was able to enjoy fighting a by-election in 1958 and the General Election of 1959. After the by-election I was short-listed for the safe seat of Bournemouth East and Christchurch but failed to secure selection. That constituted the conclusion of my attempt to enter the

House of Commons. There is a destiny, they say, that shapes our ends and I have never doubted that such limited talents as I possess have been better deployed on the bench than in Parliament.

In 1960 I moved into a small flat in Hornton Street, off High Street Kensington. It was while I was there that events occurred which set the seal upon my future life. Every barrister knows the crucial importance of becoming a tenant in a good set of chambers. "Good" in this context means, of course, chambers which are able to provide its members with sufficient briefs of the right kind to enable them to further their careers at the Bar. Chambers of this quality are much sought after. The competition for membership is stiff and the element of personal contact can be important. It was at this juncture that there came into my life Mr Samuel Lincoln. Sam was near the end of his career at the Bar when he joined me in my room at Dr Johnson's Buildings. Immediately we became firm friends. Sam was married and he and his wife Ruby lived in Hornton Court near to my flat. They had one son, the late Mr Justice Anthony Lincoln QC. Sam was an old friend of one of the great barrister's clerks of the Temple, Robert Goulden. Barrister's clerks are figures of great importance at the Bar since they act as the contact between solicitor clients and the members of chambers. They fulfil a vital role in a barrister's career and professional prospects. Robert was chief clerk to the chambers of Mr James Burge, which included such luminaries of the criminal courts as Mr Victor Durand, QC, and Mr (now Lord) Jeremy Hutchinson.

This proved to be a turning point in my career at the Bar. Barely a day passed when I was not in court. The volume of work which went into the chambers was astonishing. I quickly gained experience as a busy junior, but most importantly, when I was led by leading members of chambers, I was able to witness at close quarters the superb skills of great defending counsel. They were very different in style. Durand imposed his authority upon the jury, backed up by a fine resonant voice and massive experience of the courts. Hutchinson's advocacy was a blend of charm and subtlety I have never heard equalled. Burge was briefed mainly in licensing cases, in which his jocular style was highly effective in obtaining favourable results for his clients. I remained in those chambers for eleven years until my appointment to the Metropolitan Bench in 1972.

Having married I left my flat in Hornton Street, and on the strength of my first well paid brief, purchased a rambling old rectory in Essex. This was indeed one of those extraordinary country houses to be found in the Essex/Suffolk border area which increase in size with each succeeding century. The original house was 16th century with a substantial wing added in Victorian times to house the large brood of children which was usual during that period. The grounds were extensive, but mercifully untended, and therefore all the more appropriate for a non-gardener such as myself. We lived there for 17 years and my two children Nicholas and Elizabeth, spent their young and formative years in a country environment of tranquillity and charm. Then, once again, my life underwent radical change. I was appointed a Metropolitan Stipendiary Magistrate in 1972 and in 1978 was transferred to Bow Street.

In my early days at the Bar I had never contemplated becoming a stipendiary. Seen from the point of view of counsel's benches it seemed a rather dull and prosaic job — always dealing with small cases and having constantly to hear advocacy which, to put it mildly, was frequently not of the highest order. Several members of my chambers had become "stipes." Sam Lincoln, to whom I have already referred, urged me to put my name forward. When I did so it was with considerable hesitation. I had enjoyed the Bar and leaving it was a very considerable wrench. I was exchanging the friendliness of the robing room for the loneliness of the bench. And, as with all the big decisions in life, once made there would be no going back.

At that time the procedure for judicial appointments was much simpler than it is today. Two referees of some prominence in the law were required. In addition one was interviewed by the Secretary of the Commissions, in those days Sir Thomas Skyrme. I surmounted these hurdles successfully, and since I had received satisfactory reports on my performance as a deputy, I was duly appointed. I have to admit that at first I found the responsibility terrifying. To adjudicate upon guilt or innocence, and to have to pass sentence with so little time for consideration and nobody to consult with presented an awesome task. I wondered, for a brief period, if I had done the right thing in applying for the post. But I soon found my feet. I discovered that most of the decisions I had to make were as much to do with common sense as with law.

My first five years were spent at Thames Court in the East End of London. The River Police are the oldest branch of the London uniformed police force. The original Thames Magistrates' Court was situated in Wapping, alongside the river. In my time it had moved to Arbour Square in Whitechapel. Later still a new court was built in Bow Road, where the new building now resides. Being an East End "beak" took me back to my childhood days in that same area — a part of London for which I shall always feel a very special affection. After five years at Thames I was invited by the then Chief Magistrate, Sir Evelyn Russell, to Bow Street. The 21 years I have spent at that famous and historic court has been by far the most significant period of my life and constitutes the main part of what I have to say in this work.

Making Justice More Efficient
It is far beyond the ambit of this work to discuss in any detail those measures for the improvement of the administration of justice which have been proposed in recent years by various bodies which have been convened for the purpose, such as the Royal Commission on Criminal Procedure of 1981, the Home Office review of 1989 and the Royal Commission of 1992. Still less do I intend to go into the extent to which their proposals have been enacted in legislation or the consequences of such enactments, beneficial or otherwise.

I shall therefore confine myself to a few comments on the effects upon my work as a stipendiary resulting from a number of the manifold changes which have been introduced, the extent to which I have found these helpful, and a few suggestions I have in mind for improvement. When I say improvement I have no wish to be associated with an attitude which it seems to me is current today, namely that if something has worked well for a great many years, that is a sign that it needs to be changed. I dare say that advancing years make one more resistant to the adjustments necessitated by the transformations of time. Yet when I look back over 27 years to the day when I was appointed to the bench and ask myself whether the courts are more effectively run today than was the case I would hesitate before giving an unequivocal reply. I am however happily certain of one thing. That is the greatly reduced incidence of the bureaucratic thinking which placed so much stress upon the financial and expeditious aspect of reform that the interests of the judicial element seemed to be relegated to a subordinate position. There are certainly areas of procedure in which the public interest involves all three, but best business practice and justice do not always make good bedfellows. It was also noticeable that some of those who were most strident for change had little or no background of practical experience in the management of the courts. In the new managerial society in which we now live and have our being it is not perhaps out of place to put in a plea that those who will be managing the courts, or at least some of them, should be persons with knowledge and experience of the kind which equips them for their task.

In 1989 I was privileged to be invited to sit on the Home Office committee to review magistrates' courts' procedure. Our terms of reference were to "consider how magistrates' courts' procedure could be made more effective, efficient and economical consistent with satisfactory provision for due process."

The review's main committee was chaired by the Home Office and comprised representatives of the police, the Crown Prosecution Service, the Lord Chancellor's Department, the Justices' Clerks' Society, the Magistrates' Association, the Law Society and the Bar Council. The detailed work was carried out by seven sub-groups tasked with examining the following subjects: the initiation of process; the jurisdiction and composition of the court; the enforcement of sums adjudged to be paid; the role of the justices' clerk; the procedure at substantive hearing and the appeals process.

My own service was on the second and sixth of these. Some of our recommendations were accepted, others were not, and a few merely mirrored the practice already in existence, such as the duty of the court to assist an unrepresented defendant. Other suggestions were the service of court documents by first class post or fax, legislation to permit a magistrates' court to convict a defendant of an alternative lesser offence in certain cases, and a review of the need to give evidence on oath and the procedure to be followed.

This last matter was of special interest to me since I have believed for a long time that the oath should be abolished altogether. I adopt this position out of respect, not disrespect for the oath. My reason for coming round to this point of view is because the present form of oath is no longer effective in persuading witnesses to speak the truth. For 27 years I have sat in court listening to bare-faced lies, sometimes from one side, sometimes from the other and occasionally from both. This is something one becomes accustomed to. What I have never found easy to accept is the facile manner in which lying witnesses give their evidence after having made a solemn promise to the Almighty to tell nothing but the truth. The purpose of an oath is to impose upon an individual an obligation which is binding upon his or her conscience. It is more powerful than a mere promise or undertaking since it involves the name of God and its breach involves, for believers whatever their creed, disloyalty to the Deity and not merely to men or women. For this reason such a solemn pledge has been regarded, down the ages, as a very serious act indeed.

There are, broadly speaking, two kinds of oath. The first imposes an obligation to tell the truth. The second constitutes a pledge to perform faithfully the duties of a particular office or position. They are very different in their degree of commitment. The former is exact and precise. It makes no concession to human frailty in the form of deviation or equivocation. It commands the responsibility to tell the truth, the whole truth and nothing but the truth. It is not, as opposed to the latter, a statement of good intent.

The taking of an oath by a witness was for centuries regarded as so solemn a matter that no provision was made for an affirmation or anything of a similar character. If a person was unwilling to take the oath any evidence they might give was regarded as worthless. The extent to which times have changed can be seen in the wording of the Oaths Act 1978:

> "When an oath has been duly administered, the fact that the person to whom it was administered had at the time of taking it no religious belief does not for any purpose affect its validity."

The principle enunciated in this passage may have a practical application but it negates the whole purpose of taking an oath and reduces it to a meaningless formality.

Two things are indicative of the extent to which the "spiritual" oath, as it is sometimes called, has declined in significance. The first is the cessation of the practice, once followed in courts, of asking a witness who wishes to affirm the reason for this. The question was once put to such a witness: "Do you wish to affirm because taking an oath is contrary to your conscience or because you have no religious belief?" Nobody bothers to make this inquiry any longer. Similarly, if the holy book of the witness concerned is not available in court that witness is allowed to make an affirmation instead. The second, and more noticeable symptom of the fading importance of the oath in the public mind is the manner in which it is frequently taken today. Many witnesses, when asked their religion, merely look puzzled. The ensuing pause is generally followed by expressions such as "not much" or "not really." When a religion is selected as convenient for the occasion it is generally "C of E." If all those claiming allegiance to the Church of England in the witness box were genuine followers, the churches would be so full that it would be impossible to find a spare seat.

Worse than this is the casual off-hand way in which the words of the oath are often repeated. Frequently they are gabbled at a speed or in an indistinct manner which makes it abundantly plain that they mean nothing at all to the speaker. How can it be seriously thought for one moment that an oath has any significant effect on the truthfulness or otherwise of a witness who takes it in such a manner? The witness may in fact be truthful, but this has little to do with the swearing of an oath.

In order to discover whether there is any argument for retaining the oath it is necessary to examine its true purpose and whether or not that purpose is being fulfilled in our day and age. Promising to give truthful evidence in court where a fellow human being's reputation or liberty may be at stake is in itself a grave matter, and should induce a responsibly minded person to adhere to the truth to the best of his or her ability unless there is a very strong inducement to depart from it. The reason behind swearing by Almighty God to tell the truth is to strengthen greatly the sense of obligation to be totally honest. It is intended to make the would-be liar doubly uncomfortable about his or her dishonesty. Subject to this test how effective is the "spiritual" oath?

There is no doubt that a large number of people still maintain a belief in God. Gallup polls have shown this to be so, although such surveys reveal that for only a minority has this belief any significant influence on the way they conduct their lives. In other words, for many it is a casual acknowledgement rather than a living faith. Nevertheless, they may well take an oath based on the idea that this will add weight and veracity to their evidence. It may also be thought that magistrates and judges are establishment figures and therefore take a more benign view of a witness who swears an oath as opposed to one who affirms. This absurd view has doubtless been encouraged by those who in recent years have been engaged in a spiteful and wholly misconceived campaign to denigrate the judiciary and the magistracy of this country. In fact the very reverse is true. An affirmation, whether made for reasons of conscience which object to an oath, or through absence of belief, will often impress the tribunal because the fact that a witness feels in conscience bound not to take an oath underlines that person's integrity.

The nub of the problem, however, is that over and over again in our courts a solemn undertaking is given to the Almighty to speak the undiluted truth and what follows is a tissue of lies. An oath taken without a spark of belief in or respect for its deeper meaning and purpose, is not only a form of blasphemy. It positively detracts from, rather than adds to the solemnity of the occasion. It lowers the dignity of the judicial process.

If this is the situation with regard to witnesses there is an even greater difficulty in the case of defendants. A defendant, giving evidence on his or her own behalf is under a special kind of pressure. It is a fact of human nature that most of us, put in a tight enough corner, are capable of being "economical with the truth," to put it at its lowest. Add to that the fact that many defendants are persons with a history of dishonesty and you have all the ingredients of lies by the score being told in the witness box. It is traditional that people who lie in the witness box in their own defence are not prosecuted for perjury. Apart from any other consideration the sheer volume of cases would render this impossible. We have, therefore, a vast body of people who in addition to being dishonest, if they want to lie their way out of trouble are made perjurers, which is something even worse. The case for the abolition of the oath is based upon the acceptance of a simple but blatantly obvious fact of life: witnesses go into the witness box intending to speak the truth or determined to tell lies. In very few cases, if any, does the oath-taking process make any difference.

He or she who seeks to bring about change must have something better to offer in substitution. The Magistrates' Association has for many years expressed its dissatisfaction with the law as it stands at present, and many among the justices' clerks and solicitors branches of the legal profession take a similar view. In 1968 the Magistrates' Association resolved at their Annual General Meeting that

> "in the opinion of the Association, the oath as it is now taken in the magistrates' courts, should be replaced by a simple promise to tell the truth, the whole truth and nothing but the truth, and that breach of this promise should be perjury."

At its 1983 Annual General Meeting a resolution noted the continuing unsatisfactory state of the law regarding the oath and sought early legislation to rectify matters. The law still remains unchanged. Why is this?

The issue was considered by the Church of England authorities and that body, presided over by the Bishop of Lambeth papered over the cracks in the best Anglican style. It was said that most people still believed in God. This overlooked completely the question of to what extent such belief influenced their veracity when giving evidence. The Dean of the Arches had spoken to 20 Old Bailey judges who had favoured retaining the oath for witnesses. It was inconsistent to retain the oath for swearing in jurors but not for witnesses. On the basis of those, and other remarkable examples of logic, the meeting failed to reach a conclusion.

This author has a constructive suggestion. The "spiritual" oath should be totally abandoned. It should be replaced by an undertaking in simple and straightforward language along these lines: "I solemnly declare and promise that I will tell the truth. I am aware that if I tell a lie I am liable to be prosecuted." This formula, which threatens human as opposed to Divine retribution to the perjured witness, is better suited to the age in which we live.

On October 27, 1992, together with the then chief magistrate and his predecessor, I attended the Royal Commission on Criminal Justice to give evidence on behalf of the metropolitan bench. The three matters to which I gave voice were, first, that committal proceedings in magistrates' courts should be abolished in favour of "paper" hearings before circuit judges. Secondly, I said that I believed many "either way" offences should be made summary only and that magistrates should have their sentencing jurisdiction increased to two years for one offence and an overall maximum of four years. Thirdly, in conjunction with my colleagues I argued that confessions made in police stations should be tape-recorded and that in the absence of any such recording there must be corroboration to render such a confession admissible in evidence. All of these proposals are in the process of implementation.

Many ideas and proposals have been put forward over the years for the purpose of streamlining the procedure, accelerating the process and rationalising the methods of work in magistrates' courts. Some of these innovations, when put into effect, have significantly failed to achieve any of these objectives. It has sometimes, in my view, resembled a game in which a group of people have to search for buried treasure. Everyone is entitled to make intelligent suggestions as to where the treasure might be found, but the person who actually discovers it is disqualified for having spoilt the game.

The introduction of "section 6(2)" or "paper" committals has undoubtedly been beneficial in saving court time but this has been largely negated by the continuance, prior to their being completely phased out, of the section 6(1) and "old style" hearings in which witnesses can be called and cross-examined. This has been the real "villain of the piece" where court time has been concerned. The process by which the defence have had the right to what in effect is a preliminary trial when there is no reasonable chance of the case for the prosecution being dismissed at that stage has always impressed me as a ludicrous waste of time. The recently introduced transfer provisions have been effective in avoiding the more absurd situations. There are no submissions for the defence which are made in the magistrates' court which cannot be equally well made in the Crown Court. The great expansion of the latter tribunal during the 1970s and 1980s would be more fully justified if all committal proceedings without qualification are speedily removed from the jurisdiction of magistrates.

Another problem which has beset magistrates' courts is that of the "either way" offence. Here the defendant has the choice of agreeing to be dealt with by the magistrates' court, or electing to be tried by a judge and jury. Under the new procedure if a plea of guilty is entered the magistrate has jurisdiction. Research done for the Royal Commission showed that 27 per cent of those electing trial intended from the outset to plead guilty. At the time of the trial 23 per cent had pleaded guilty to some or all of the charges. Half of those electing trial at the Crown Court believed, mistakenly, that they would obtain a lighter sentence at that court. A report published by the Home Secretary in 1997 recommended that the automatic right to elect jury trial should be withdrawn in a whole range of cases including assault, causing actual bodily harm, indecency, theft and burglaries. However, the General Election of that year put paid to these proposals—yet similar proposals are now being discussed by a government of a different political complexion.

The concern of the Royal Commission was that defendants should not be able to "play the system." Proposal 114 stated:

> "In cases involving either way offences the defendant should no longer have the right to insist on a trial by jury. Where the CPS and the defendant agree that the case is suitable for summary trial, it should proceed to trial in a magistrates' court. The case should go to the Crown Court for trial if both prosecution and defence agree that it should be tried on indictment. Where the defence do not agree with the CPS's proposal on which court should try the case, the matter should be referred to the magistrates for a decision."

Proposal 118 further stated:

"In indictable only cases submissions of no case to answer should be decided by the Crown Court. In either way cases the responsibility should fall to the magistrates' courts, where Stipendiary Magistrates should preside over the hearings."

These are, in the view of this author, wise provisions which could be followed with advantage. The James Committee tackled the problem many years ago, recommending that a defendant should no longer have the right to trial by jury for any offence for which the maximum sentence did not exceed six months. It recommended that the maximum sentence for a number of offences, including driving under the influence of drink, should be reduced to six months. These suggestions were enacted in the Criminal Law Act 1977. By common consent the consequence was greater justice rather than injustice. Yet, with Crown Court cases costing up to ten times as much as those in magistrates' courts there remains much unfinished business in this area. Is our system of justice still too heavily weighted in favour of the defence? In my view it still is. I have endeavoured, over my 27 years on the bench to avoid becoming cynical, and I believe I have succeeded. But I have not abandoned realism, and I feel sure that at least 50 per cent of defendants who plead not guilty are in fact guilty as charged. The proportion may in reality be a great deal higher. How to create conditions in which the guilty are more likely to be convicted but without prejudice to the innocent? It is a jurisprudential problem of great difficulty. A submission by the Metropolitan Stipendiary Magistrates to the Royal Commission, which I would endorse, is that where a defendant is legally represented the defence should at least provide an outline of its case to the prosecution, and that this should apply at all levels of criminal courts. Such a provision would extend the principle of advance disclosure to include both prosecution and defence.[1] This seems to me to be a fair concept. Another proposal put forward by the body to which I belong was that previous convictions for similar

---

1. Something that has since been implemented.

offences should be admitted to prove the guilty mind (*mens rea*) of a defendant where the act itself (*actus reus*) is admitted by him. This, it was submitted, could result in the conviction of guilty persons who are at present acquitted, but not of innocent persons.

After conviction, further issues arise. As a stipendiary magistrate I have a wide variety of alternatives to imprisonment at my disposal. What is crucial about community sentences is that they are not seen as a soft option. I have always appreciated the negative value of locking people away in prison for comparatively minor offences, but I am sometimes dismayed at the frequency with which community sentences appear on an offender's record, followed by further crime. My suggestion would be that probation orders, community service orders and combination orders should be accompanied by a suspended sentence of imprisonment which would descend like the "Sword of Damocles" for any deliberate breach of or unwillingness to comply with the order. This would retain the constructive element in such sentencing while at the same time compelling greater respect for the court.

I think there is a case for a more draconian attitude towards fine defaulters. There are, of course, circumstances in which the imposition of a fine is a ludicrous penalty. When sitting on Saturday morning means inquiries, I have been confronted with absurd situations in which penniless people have been ordered to pay substantial sums at the rate of £1 a week, or even less. But the lack of firm evidence of income frequently enables offenders to play the court along and to contribute to the enormous back-log of unpaid fines, much of which has to be written off.

The courts have been increasingly discouraged from imposing imprisonment on fine defaulters and I can see the logic of this. But in my view the courts should have discretion, in appropriate cases, to back up a financial penalty with a custodial sentence at an earlier stage than is at present permitted.

Finally, a word about police cautions. Let me say that I have always been doubtful about the recently heralded policy of policing called "zero tolerance." I am aware of the claims that have been made of remarkable results when this policy has been followed, both here and in America. I do suspect however, that the tendency created is for crime to be shifted from one area to another, or perhaps to be temporarily suppressed. At the same time I think the practice of cautioning offenders instead of prosecuting them must be followed with circumspection.

At the start of the present decade police forces throughout the country were urged to caution more adult offenders in a move to keep them out of the court system and so to reduce the risk of re-offending. The practice of cautioning juveniles has been commonplace since a study in 1983 showed that fewer were likely to re-offend than was the case with those who were prosecuted. But statistics are rarely conclusive and in spite of a greatly increased number of young offenders being cautioned findings of guilt in the older age groups increased.

There are a number of arguments in favour of cautioning. As an alternative to prosecution it avoids the necessity and expense of bringing defendants before the courts. This is especially important when the offender is a young person or, in the case of an adult, an elderly, sick or mentally impaired individual. It reduces the number of trivial offences taking up judicial time and relieves pressure on the ever growing lists in magistrates' courts. For the same reasons it lightens the burden on probation officers and saves a great deal of police time and involvement. Although cautions are cited in court they do not amount to a conviction, and hence the cautioned party does not acquire a criminal record. In addition to these considerations a formal caution puts "teeth" into what would otherwise be a mere warning.

There is not, and never has been, a rule of law that suspect persons must be prosecuted, but cautioning has special significance in the case of juveniles because of the necessity, where possible, of keeping children out of the criminal justice system. The Parliamentary All-Party Penal Affairs Group in 1981 endorsed the view of the Black Committee which stressed that the cautioning of young offenders is not a soft option, but rather a positive response to delinquency, aiming to help and encourage children to channel their natural energy into legitimate activities. The committee set out four factors with this aim in mind. First, if the child is not a persistent delinquent he or she may mature out of the offending phase. Secondly, the impact of a police warning in a formal setting may be sufficient to deter further offending. Thirdly, the child's family will be alerted to the situation, and fourthly, references to concerned agencies will enable those bodies to assist in dealing with factors in the child's life which have contributed to the trouble.

The police would appear to have a complete discretion as to whether or not to caution. Factors for consideration are the gravity of the offence and the offender's record. A first offender can normally expect a caution and likewise a second if the matter is not serious. There have been wide variations in cautioning rates and procedures between police forces. Concern has also been expressed about the effectiveness of repeated cautions. Another obvious question is how the interests of the victim can be protected? Courts are required to give reasons if compensation is not awarded, but there is no power at all to order any kind of compensation if the offender merely has a caution. Should the victim's consent to a caution be required in cases of personal injury or damage to or loss of property? Is there a danger that offences which are too serious will qualify for cautioning?

Perhaps the greatest concern for the courts is the prospect of a burgeoning area of extra-judicial justice. Crimes are committed over which the courts have no jurisdiction because the police decide to take no action other than to warn the offender not to do it again.

These are matters of interest which I raise. They may be the subject of discussion long after I have left the bench.

CHAPTER 11

Japanese Days

This chapter is more autobiographical than the others in this book, apart from the one entitled "A Little of Myself"! This is because it concerns a chapter in my life which has been of the utmost importance to me. It has been, and still is, a very happy period because it stems from the fact that in 1981 I married my wife, Hisako, who is Japanese, and is a wonderful partner and companion.

The high standards of honesty in Japan were brought home to me on my arrival at Narita airport. We had been driving towards the family home for about an hour when to my dismay I discovered that, in one of those moments of absent-mindedness which have been the bane of my life, I had left my suitcase behind. If all the coats, hats, umbrellas and brief-cases I have inadvertently abandoned on various forms of transport were collected together they would, I feel sure, stock a sizeable department store. After yet another hour's drive we arrived back at Narita to find that my case was precisely where I had left it—an event which might be less likely to occur at, say, King's Cross.

The spirits of ancestors are a real presence for many Japanese.

Shinto, the ancient religion of Japan and Buddhism, a later arrival from India and China, exist harmoniously side by side on the religious scene in Japan. Christianity is a minority religion. There are roughly a million baptised Christians more or less equally divided between Roman Catholics and Protestants.

It had been my intention, during a fairly short stay, to see places of interest and to make contact with people in the criminal justice system. With this in view Hisako and I took the "bullet" train to the ancient imperial city of Kyoto. It was the first time I had ever experienced a ticket collector raising his hat to me before checking my ticket! At Kyoto we visited a great many temples and shrines. The structures were of timber and impressed one by the atmosphere of peace and tranquillity which pervaded the inner rooms. Yet there appeared to be no central symbol of worship such as the altar in a Christian church or cathedral. The surrounding gardens were always beautiful and invariably followed the traditional design of water, shrubbery and rock. Kyoto was once the imperial city of Japan before Tokyo rose to prominence. The Imperial Gardens were especially attractive with the coloured tints of the bushes, the lush green undergrowth and the streams passing among the rocks and transversed in places by small oriental bridges. We visited such places of interest as the Temple of Shugakuin and saw the great hall with 1001 golden figures of the Buddha and, later on, the giant Buddha of Nara.

It had been my intention on this first visit to Japan to meet and exchange views with members of the Japanese legal professions. I was invited to the Ministry of Justice in Tokyo where I met the head of the Criminal Justice Division and other members of the staff. At Tokyo I spoke to a mixed Japanese and European audience at the British Council Centre on the subject of The Life and Work of a London Stipendiary Magistrate. I delivered a similar lecture to students at the Ritsumeikan University in Kyoto. Subsequently we travelled to Osaka where I delivered a lecture to the Law Society there. Wherever I went I was greatly impressed with the complete absence of street crime in Japanese cities and the obvious safety with which it was possible to walk around at all hours of the night without any qualms about one's safety.

The Japanese have a national police force. An experiment on a more local level was unsuccessful: it did not measure up to the standards of efficiency that are aimed at in that country. Hence, overall supervision of the police is under direct central government control. The highest body is the National Public Safety Commission, which consists of a chairman and five members, each appointed by the Prime Minister for a five-year term with the agreement of both houses of the Diet (parliament). The chairman must be a state Minister, answerable to the Prime Minister. The Commission presides over police training, communications, administration and equipment, and deals with natural disasters and civil disturbances and all matters of national public safety. This contrasts

Japanese Days

with our own system of chief constables, answerable to some extent, to their local police authorities.[1]

Below the National Public Safety Commission comes the National Police Agency: the second is, in effect, the executive arm of the first, putting its decisions into operation down to local level, and working out the detailed planning required. This agency, under a director-general, operates through five bureaux, each of which controls a major area of police work; through these authority is channelled via regional bureaux to the 47 prefectural police departments in Japan.

The population of Japan is about 120 million and the strength of the police about 215,000 officers, so there is a ratio of one policeman to 550 people. The largest concentration of police is, of course, the Tokyo Metropolitan Police Department. Like the police of America and Western Europe the Japanese police are armed, but there are specialist departments to deal with specific situations. Membership of the special police, as opposed to the patrol police — calls for exceptional ability and physical fitness. This is especially true of the *Kidotai*, the riot police units. The fact that they assist in all kinds of emergency, coupled with the natural love of order endemic in the Japanese character, means that this quasi-military force of 15,000 is a source of pride rather than dislike. Indeed, in Japan the police enjoy the support and confidence of the population generally. This is largely due to the excellent relations which exist at local level between police and people.

The area of each prefecture is divided into districts, in every one of which there is a police station (*Keisatsu-Sho*). This is manned by up to 500 officers, according to the locality. At a lower level of organization, there are established police-boxes. These are normally manned by two police officers, serving in rotation.

Great importance is placed upon community relations. There are numerous civilian groups which encourage citizen partnerships with police in the battle with crime. Some of these are powerful organizations which exist to support the police financially, socially and in other ways. The police, for their part, are every bit as industrious as our own

---

1. Now in England and Wales chief constables answer to elected police and crime commissioners.

in striving for good police-citizen relationships, and in educating the public in methods of crime prevention. For example, Japanese police authorities have designated 85 zones as "theft prevention areas" based on a high theft rate in each. Joint patrols by police officers and residents, the distribution of crime prevention leaflets, community meetings and the voluntary inspection of homes to make criminal entry more difficult have achieved a reduction in the theft rate of 20 per cent in these districts.

The qualifications to become a judge, a public prosecutor or a privately practising lawyer are the same in each case in Japan. Candidates must pass the National Bar Examination, complete two years of training and pass the final examination. After that they choose their career in the law.

Public prosecutors are appointed by the Minister of Justice, but they also enjoy substantial independence because under the law, with regard to the disposal of individual cases, the Minister of Justice may only direct and supervise the Prosecutor-General, who is the head of career public prosecutors.

Article 1 of the Code of Criminal Procedure of 1948 states that the basic principle underlying investigation and trial is

> "to clarify the true facts of cases and to apply and realise criminal laws or ordinances fairly and speedily, while thoroughly accomplishing the maintenance of public welfare and the security of fundamental human rights of individuals."

The stated effect of this is that while the principle of "substantive truth" is adopted, the civil liberty of the suspect and accused (under Japanese law the alleged offender is termed "the suspect" before prosecution and "the accused" thereafter, until conviction or acquittal) is preserved.

Japan does not have investigation by an examining magistrate as on the European continent, nor does it employ a grand jury system as found in the United States of America. The main investigating authorities are the police and the public prosecutors, and the mode of criminal trial, as in this country, is adversarial. As to the purpose of the criminal investigation procedure I quote my friend Mr Seiji Kurata at that time Director of the Legislative Affairs Division of the Criminal Affairs Bureau of the Ministry of Justice in Tokyo:

> "The most notable feature of criminal investigation in Japan is that the utmost effort is made to liberate those suspects who might be acquitted if prosecuted, and those offenders who need not be punished, from the burden of the criminal process at the earliest opportunity. The sole purpose of this effort is to protect the civil liberty of the suspect. Thus, in Japan, the investigation authorities not only try to collect evidence sufficient to secure a conviction including evidence to rebut every possible defence, but also try to find evidence to exonerate the suspect. At the same time the investigating authorities gather all information and materials relevant to assess the gravity of the offence and the circumstances of the offender. In short, criminal investigation by the police and public prosecutors in Japan may be said to cover nearly the same extent as is covered by the combination of investigation by an examining judge in the continental law jurisdictions and the pre-sentence investigation prevalent in the Anglo-American legal systems."

Investigation in criminal cases is normally initiated by the police who refer the case to the public prosecutor who in turn gives the police instructions as to the course of action to take and decides whether or not to prosecute.

The maximum period of custody before the decision whether to prosecute or not is 23 days. If the public prosecutor does not make a decision within that period the suspect must be released.

Once the public prosecutor is satisfied that he or she has enough evidence to prove the guilt of the suspect, then he or she has unfettered discretion in deciding how to dispose of the case. If the case is a very serious one where the offender is deserving of imprisonment the public prosecutor will prosecute for what is termed "formal trial."

The prosecutor, unlike in our own system, can recommend that the court opt for a sentence of imprisonment. This only applies, however, in a very small percentage of cases. The majority of criminal cases are dealt with as summary trials.

In Japan a high proportion of offenders admit their guilt. If in such a situation the offence is relatively minor and the offender is penitent the public prosecutor will interview the defendant and also family and friends. If the case has been settled privately, for example by the payment of compensation, and the offender has apologised to the victim, and also if the family and friends of the offender are willing to help him or her to rehabilitate himself or herself, the public prosecutor may decide to grant "suspension of prosecution"—that is, not to prosecute.

In Japan there are no jury trials or trials by lay justices. All cases are tried by professional Judges. At the trial court level serious cases are tried by a three-Judge court and others are tried by a one-Judge court. The burden of proof is entirely on the prosecution. The concept of a *prima facie* case is unknown in Japan. The hearsay rule does, however, apply, unless the other party consents to its admission.

There is no division of the proceedings into trial and sentencing. Consequently matters such as previous convictions, the victim's feelings and opinions, the degree of remorse shown by the defendant and any restitution already made are heard by the court.

The acquittal rate is extremely low. This is partly because more than 90 per cent of indicted people plead guilty, and also the fact that public prosecutors refrain from prosecuting if there is any possibility of an acquittal.

In Japan both prosecution and defence have the right to appeal twice; first to one of the eight high courts against conviction, acquittal or sentence, and secondly, to the Supreme Court if the decision by the lower court contradicts the Constitution or the precedents of the Supreme Court. Article 31 of the Constitution provides that

> "no person shall be deprived of life or liberty, nor shall any other criminal penalty be imposed, except according to procedure established by law", while Article 33 states that "no person shall be arrested except upon warrant issued by a competent judicial officer, which specifies the offence with which the person is charged, unless he is arrested in the commission of the offences."

Further, as prescribed in Article 34,

"no person shall be detained or confined without being at once informed of the charge against him, or without the immediate privilege of counsel. Nor shall he be confined without adequate cause and, upon demand of any person, such cause must be immediately shown in open court in his presence and the presence of his counsel."

Other articles provide citizens with protection against the unlawful entry and search of their homes, the improper obtaining of confessions, and undue delay before being brought to trial.

All this is familiar reading to those who know the English law, and the rules about arrests with and without warrant are very similar to our own. After arrest, the police must immediately release a suspect if they believe there is no urgent need to detain him. If there is such a need, the police must take steps to transfer the suspect to the police prosecutor's office, together with all the evidence obtained, within 48 hours of arrest. Further stringent rules govern the period of time during which the public prosecutor must submit evidence before the judge or release the accused. The grounds upon which the judge may order the continued detention of the accused make an interesting comparison with the Bail Act. This power arises when either (1) the defendant has no fixed abode; (2) there are reasonable grounds for suspecting that he may destroy evidence, or (3) there is reason to suspect that he may escape the jurisdiction.

The efficiency and record of Japan's criminal system are impressive. It would, I believe, be unfair and perhaps betray an unworthy hint of envy to suggest that because of the nature of Japanese society, the police have a comparatively easy task. Nor is there the slightest evidence that they possess powers which enable them to ride roughshod over fundamental human rights. Nevertheless, there is undoubtedly much in the Japanese character which makes for law and order. The strength of the family with its code of honour; the homogeneous nature of the population and the general sense of discipline provide an environment which is favourable to the implementation of criminal justice.

Nagasaki

The place is as beautiful as the name. A lovely little harbour town, bustling with life and activity, which appealed to me immensely when I visited it and which made a lasting impression upon my mind. Yet it was here, on August 9, 1945 at 11.10 am that one of the most terrible events in history, matched only by the devastation in Hiroshima three days earlier, took place. I stood in Peace Park, next to the stone obelisk which marks the epicentre of the explosion. It was an eerie and uncomfortable sensation to know that had I occupied that precise spot 40 years earlier I would have been evaporated. Death is the same, however it comes, but when surrounded by the ritual of a funeral service, within the dignified atmosphere of an array of flowers, hymns and sorrowing friends and relatives, there is a personal factor which gives some meaning to the life of the departed. But to simply disappear into thin air is a brutally abrupt end to existence. Yet compared with many of the survivors of that apocalyptic horror the dead could be considered the lucky ones. But that was long in the past when I came to Nagasaki.

My wife and I were met at the airport by a lady, Shigeko, who had been a friend of my wife's in college days. Thus, after booking in at our hotel, we enjoyed the advantage of being guided to places of interest by someone who lived in the town. Indeed, there was much to see and appreciate. Nagasaki, due to its position, was one of the first Japanese cities to experience western influence. Partly for this reason its history is both colourful and traumatic.

It was to this part of Japan that the Jesuit missionaries came in the 16th century under the inspiration of St Francis Xavier. They made impressive progress in converting the Japanese to the faith, so impressive that violent reaction eventually took place. Until comparatively modern times the most powerful figure in Japan was the shogun. The Emperor was at that time a figurehead, albeit one with divine credentials. It was upon the orders of the shogun that a widespread persecution of the Christians began. We visited a castle containing relics of the period. Among these was the fumie. This is a brass impression of the face of Christ. The inquisitors would line up the inhabitants of a village and order them to trample on the fumier. Those who refused or hesitated were identified

Japanese Days

as members of the Christian community and singled out for torture, or death if they refused to apostatise. In the grounds of the castle was the scene of a pitched battle in which the Christians, led by a teenage boy whose statue venerates his memory, made a last stand against the forces of the shogun.

We visited Jesuit churches, in one of which we saw a huge painting of the rows of crosses on which the martyrs hung, and later, on the same theme, stayed at Unzen in the mountains and saw the hot sulphurous mountain streams into which those who refused to abandon their faith, were thrown. The church was suppressed, but survived in secrecy and silence until freedom of worship was restored in Japan. The history of the period has been brilliantly portrayed by the Japanese writer Shusako Endo. Not very long after our stay at Unzen a nearby volcano erupted and much of the area where we had been was covered in molten lava.

On a lighter note, we paid a call at the allegedly original house of Madame Butterfly on whose tragic fate the opera by Pucini was based. And then on to the home of Thomas Blake Glover. This was something which gave me a very real sense of national pride. Thomas Blake Glover was one of that extraordinary generation of Victorian English the like of which this country has never produced before or since. He arrived in Nagasaki in the mid-19th century with little except his own commanding personality. He married a Japanese woman and they had the typically large family. True to his generation Glover was a creator and a constructor. He designed and constructed railroads and a telegraph system. He busied himself in many activities, enrolling local people in his support and overcoming all obstacles. His self-confidence, true to his Victorian credentials, was absolute. In the house were life-sized effigies of the family. Perhaps the most moving was the scene at a dinner table. At the head was Blake Glover, his hand extended as he offered up grace. At the opposite end of the table sat his wife. Along one side sit the children and opposite them two Samurai warriors. All have their heads appropriately bowed in reverence for the occasion. Blake Glover's resting place is in the garden. His bust with its Victorian side-whiskers surmounts the tomb on which is inscribed the date on which he was laid to rest and his award of the Order of the Rising Sun for his services to Japan. I left that place feeling a little proud to be British.

Near the harbour itself was the quarter of the city which had been the home of the Dutch traders. It possessed the unmistakable atmosphere of that country.

I felt that it was mandatory to visit the Museum of the Atomic Bomb. I knew that I was in for a grim experience. I was right in so thinking. There will always be debate over the decision of President Truman to authorise the use of this terrible weapon of mass destruction. The view that this was merely a further escalation of the weaponry of modern warfare is far too facile. This really was different. For the first time in history the human race was put on notice of the fact that its annihilation is a possibility.

It has been said that the enormous expenditure of $2 billion — at 1945 values — had to be justified. One hopes that this is untrue. The thought that such an ocean of suffering could possibly be based upon financial considerations is too dreadful to contemplate. Military experts have differed over the necessity of dropping the atomic bomb. Some point to the fact that Japan was already defeated, and of this there can be no doubt. Her navy had been sunk and her industry destroyed. Peace feelers were being put out by persons in government. Yet it is clear that the military fanatics who ruled Japan would have had none of this. For them war meant victory or death, and if the outcome was death, then so be it. The Americans had learnt the cost of fighting a desperately courageous opponent at Okinawa. This island, well to the south of mainland Japan, was defended with surpassing bravery. The Kamikaze pilots, by diving their explosive-filled planes onto the American ships had already done so much damage that the Americans were considering calling off the invasion. In capturing the island itself American casualties ran to 30,000 dead and wounded. The price of an invasion of the mainland had only to be imagined.

For a conventional invasion of Japan proper the United States government had earmarked 750,000 troops and marines. Japan still had 1,000,000 soldiers under arms and a civilian volunteer force of 20,000,000, all of whom were pledged to die for the Emperor. In addition to this was the fact that Japan, being two-thirds mountainous terrain, would have lent itself to guerrilla warfare which might have dragged on long after formal hostilities had ceased and cost many more American lives.

Then there was the political dimension. Stalin had made it clear that he wanted Japan divided between the victorious allies as had been done with Germany and Austria. Japan, which is close to Russia and a long way from America, would have suffered a tripartite occupation. This would have been to the liking of the large and vociferous Communist party which existed in Japan at the end of the war, but the consequences for the Japanese people, political and economic, would have been dire indeed.

The alternative was to force a rapid conclusion by the use of the bomb. The President of the United States is not merely First Executive of that nation, he is also Commander-in-Chief of the armed forces. The question must in fairness be asked: should a commander, in time of war, make a decision which is more favourable to his own side or to that of the enemy?

Modern war is total. Everyone, men, women and children are inevitable targets. This I felt had to be borne in mind when I entered the Atomic Bomb Memorial Museum in Nagasaki. Yet what I saw seemed to have special significance and a particular horror. The scientists who constructed the device were breaking new ground. They did not anticipate the effects of radioactivity on the human body, or the fact that those effects can be transmitted from one generation to another. The ground floor of the building consisted of objects which demonstrated the heat and blast of the bomb. There was a clock whose face had been smashed in with the hands forever fixed at the moment of the explosion. There was a solid rock melted by the heat. An interesting feature was a message in a cylinder sent by an American scientist to one of his Japanese counterparts warning of the imminent use of new and terrible weapon. Alas, the message fell into the wrong hands. Nagasaki was unlucky. The plane which flew from Okinawa, had targeted another town further to the north, but that place was obscured by cloud. On its return the plane passed over Nagasaki, and since the town was visible through a break in the clouds, dropped the bomb there. The bomb descended by parachute, exploding at a height destined to have maximum effect. This effect was emphasised by the fact that Nagasaki is surrounded by mountains which contained the blast, already travelling at an unprecedented speed.

On the first floor of the museum one saw the fearful human costs. I remember as a schoolboy aged 16 sitting reading the newspapers in a tea shop. I saw the words, "Second atomic bomb hits Nagasaki." It meant nothing to me. War dehumanises the enemy. It has to. Thinking of them as one's fellow human beings would not do at all. But now I had married into a charming Japanese family and had a Japanese wife whom I loved, and things were different. The photos were deeply moving. Babes in arms with facial nuclear burns; children with the flesh scorched from their backs; a group of young women sitting around drinking water from bottles in a vain attempt to quell the fire in their bodies—all to die within minutes. One does not continue. On the top floor were murals in a similar style to Picasso's Guernica. A tape was running on which were recorded the voices of the dying, the injured and the bereaved. Perhaps this was the most harrowing of the whole exhibition.

We said farewell to our friend and headed back to the airport. As we flew out I looked down on such a different scene from the one I had viewed an hour or two before; the busy, bustling streets; the smiling faces of friends chatting; the neat, clean children playing happily as children do the world over; the surrounding hills, no longer a death trap but a beautiful back drop to a lovely place, and the whole warmed in glorious Japanese sunshine. Then I found myself thinking: if Nagasaki can do it, then maybe, just maybe, the world can do it too.

CHAPTER 12

The Pinochet Drama

During my 20 years at Bow Street there have been many interesting, and a few notable, cases in which I have been privileged to play a part. This has frequently been so in extradition. But never has there been a case with such repercussions on an international scale as that of Augusto Pinochet Ugarte, the former dictator of Chile, or with such profound consequences in terms of dissent at the highest levels of the judiciary, nor with such explosive political potential for the British government. My own role was to set the proceedings in motion in that I issued the warrant upon the authority of which General, but by then Senator, Pinochet was placed under arrest. I had never before, in the discharge of my responsibilities, ordered the arrest of so internationally prominent a personality, but the real importance of the case consists not merely in General Pinochet's position as a former head of state, but in the immensely serious and far-reaching implications for international law and the law of extradition to which the matter gave rise. Since, therefore, this case is of importance reaching far beyond the province of law and lawyers I propose to deal with it at some length. However, let me emphasise at the very beginning that my personal position is entirely neutral and based purely upon the legal issues at stake. I adopt no political stance, nor do I express any view as to the veracity or otherwise of the allegations made against Pinochet regarding the acts said to have been committed with his knowledge and consent, and even under his instructions, during his time in power.

Since the end of the Second World War there has been a steady development in that area of international law which relates to the trial and punishment of persons charged with crimes against humanity. Prior to that time little had been done to bring to book alleged perpetrators of atrocities. After the First World War a cry went up of "hang the

Kaiser" but nothing came of it, nor were reports of German barbarities in Belgium investigated. Only with the revelations in 1945 of Nazi genocide did the necessity of punishing, so far as that was possible, those responsible, become mandatory. The Nuremberg Tribunal was the first of its kind, and was matched by similar trials in Tokyo. Sadly, the Nazi holocaust did not mark the end of genocidal massacres committed by ruling regimes against their own citizens, and since those in power were frequently directly responsible, care was taken in the setting up of tribunals to deal with such outrages to ensure that nobody could escape justice by pleading state immunity. This applied to heads of state or any official, however highly placed. Article 6 of the Nuremberg Charter in 1945 gave jurisdiction to try crimes against peace, war crimes and crimes against humanity. Article 7 states,

> "the official position of defendants, whether as Heads of State or responsible officials in Government Departments shall not be considered as freeing them from responsibility or mitigating punishment."

The Tokyo Convention contained a similar provision. The international tribunal for the former Yugoslavia was given power to prosecute persons for certain crimes against humanity "when committed in armed conflict whether international or internal in character, and directed against any civilian population." Article 7 provides that "the official position of any accused person whether as Head of State or Government or as a responsible Government Official shall not relieve such person of criminal responsibility." The same clause is contained in the 1994 Statute of the International Tribunal for Rwanda.

Retribution for crimes against humanity has been placed on a more regular and permanent basis by the Rome Statute of the International Court which provides for jurisdiction in respect of genocide, as defined, and crimes against humanity, as defined, with respect to crimes committed after the coming into force of the statute. The statute provides that official capacity as a Head of State or government shall in no case exempt the person concerned from criminal responsibility.

It is very important to distinguish between the establishment of international tribunals for the trial and sentencing of those guilty of genocide and related crimes, and extradition, which is a completely different procedure. I have touched upon this subject in a previous chapter but I mention it now to emphasise the distinction between the two judicial processes. Extradition, which has a much older history than the laws of crimes against humanity, is the method by which one state applies to another for the return of a fugitive offender who has committed an extraditable crime within its jurisdiction and has fled that jurisdiction to the requested state. It is not, and never has been, a system intended to deal with crimes committed for political purposes by governments or government agents carried out within their own territories nor was it ever intended to infringe the principle that one state should not interfere in the sovereign internal affairs of another. Extradition is designed to facilitate the arrest of criminals who have committed serious crimes and who seek to escape their just desserts by decamping to another country. It is based upon relations between individual states rather than international tribunals, and these relations are contained in either *ad hoc* arrangements/treaties, or a convention such as the European Convention under the terms of which the return of General Pinochet was sought.

I will now turn to the extraordinary narrative of events which have made history and have certainly made a contribution to the long and colourful story of Bow Street Court.

The historical background to General Pinochet's acquisition of power was widely reported at the time and is only of interest in the present legal context in so far as it relates to the issue of state immunity. The story begins on September 11, 1973 when, after a successful military coup against the Marxist regime of President Allende, General Pinochet assumed power in Chile. That same day he was appointed President of the ruling military junta. On September 22 the new regime in Chile was recognised by Her Majesty's government. By decree dated December 11, 1974 General Pinochet assumed the title of President of the Republic. A new constitution came into force in Chile approved of by a national referendum in 1980. This provided for executive power in Chile to be exercised by the President of the Republic as Head of State. This remained the position until December 1989 when democratic elections were held, following which, in March 1990, General Pinochet handed over power to President Aylwin. General Pinochet was granted immunity from proceedings for acts done during his period of office and was made a senator for life. He had been Head of State during the whole period of the allegations against him.

General Pinochet had proved himself to be well-disposed towards Britain when, during the Falklands War, he made bases in Chile available to this country thereby assisting in the prosecution of the war against Argentina. Subsequently he made several private visits to England on which occasions he was accorded the respect due to him in his new role as a senator in a foreign government. On one such occasion he took tea with Mrs Thatcher, Prime Minister during the Falklands conflict. All the greater must have been his surprise and shock when, while lying in the London Clinic following an operation on his back, he found himself under arrest. This resulted from the issue by Spain on October 16, 1998 of an international warrant of arrest alleging crimes by the Pinochet government against Spanish citizens in Chile during the currency of that regime. On that same day application was made to my Bow Street colleague, Mr Nicholas Evans, for a provisional warrant to arrest Mr Pinochet. It is important here to refer to the nature of extradition warrants. Section 8 of the 1989 Extradition Act prescribes two procedures. The first is conditional upon receipt by the court of the Secretary of State's authority to proceed. The second is a provisional warrant which is not conditional upon an authority to proceed and is normally requested by the Extradition Squad when there is a danger of the fugitive leaving the jurisdiction, and hence time is of the essence. The position of the Bow Street magistrate (this being the special jurisdiction of that court) in the latter situation is set out in section 8 subsection (3) of the Act:

> "A person empowered to issue warrants of arrest under this section may issue such a warrant if he is supplied with such evidence or…information as would in his opinion justify the issue of a warrant for the arrest of a person accused or, as the case may be, convicted within his jurisdiction and

it appears to him that the conduct alleged would constitute an extradition crime."

I should perhaps apologise to my non-lawyer readers for dwelling upon the technical aspects of the law involved. I do so because in this as in other cases of public interest the press reportage can be so inaccurate, over-simplified and misleading that clarification of the legal issues is necessary.

The first provisional warrant was based on the allegation that Pinochet "Between September 11, 1973 and December 31, 1983 within the jurisdiction of the Fifth Central Magistrate of the National Court of Madrid did murder Spanish citizens in Chile within the jurisdiction of the government of Spain." The Divisional Court held that this warrant was bad because the murder of Spanish citizens in Chile was not and never had been an extradition crime. The murder of a British citizen by a non-British citizen outside the United Kingdom would not constitute an offence in respect of which the United Kingdom could claim extra-territorial jurisdiction.

The second warrant was issued by myself on October 22, 1998. I issued this warrant on the basis that there was evidence that Senator Pinochet was accused

> "Between January 1, 1988 and December 1992 being a public official intentionally inflicted severe pain or suffering on another in the performance or purported performance of his official duties within the jurisdiction of the government of Spain."

Also that

> "(1) Between January 1, 1988 and December 31, 1992, being a public official, conspired with persons unknown, to intentionally inflict severe pain or suffering on another in the performance or purported performance of his official duties;

Between January 1, 1982 and January 31, 1992 (a) he detained (b) he conspired with persons unknown to detain other persons ("the hostages") and in order to compel such persons to do or to abstain from doing any act, threatened to kill, injure or continue to detain the hostages;

Between January 1976 and December 1992, conspired with persons unknown to commit murder in a Convention country."

This last was ruled out by the Divisional Court.

At the time of his arrest under this second, valid, warrant, Pinochet was in the London Clinic. For a considerable period he had been visiting this country unmolested.

The Spanish application for his extradition was made under the European Convention of 1957 to which both Britain and Spain were signatories. I have dealt with this subject in another chapter of this book. On October 26 application was made by lawyers on behalf of Senator Pinochet for *habeas corpus* and judicial review of the warrant which I had issued. These applications were heard by the Divisional Court presided over by the Lord Chief Justice on October 26 and 27, 1998. Various matters were raised and ruled upon by the court, but the central and most crucial issue was that of sovereign immunity. Put in a nutshell the issue argued before the Divisional Court was whether the actions of General Pinochet, allegedly committed while he was Chilean Head of State, could properly be the subject of an order for his extradition. The information relevant to this question, which was supplied by Chile, was to the effect that the respondent was "President of the Government Junta of Chile" from September 11, 1973 until June 26, 1974 and "Head of State of the Republic of Chile" from June 26, 1974 until March 11, 1990. It was emphasised by the Lord Chief Justice in his full and detailed judgment that from the earliest date in the provisional warrant which I had issued, namely January 1976, General Pinochet was Head of State and had ceased to be such before January 1992 which was the latest date referred to therein. There was nothing in any document seen by the court which alleged any conduct complained of after he had ceased to be Head of State in March 1990. It was conceded on behalf of the Spanish Government that nothing said to have been done after the general ceased to be Head of Sate in March 1990 was relied upon in furtherance of his extradition.

The Lord Chief Justice then reviewed the case advanced on behalf of the general: "The applicant's proposition, put simply, is that a court in the United Kingdom will not exert criminal or civil jurisdiction over a former Head of State of a foreign country in relation to any act done in the exercise of sovereign power." This proposition, though simply stated, has tremendous implications for international relations. Counsel for the general had cited section 1 of the State Immunity Act 1978: "A state is immune from the jurisdiction of the courts of the United Kingdom except as provided in the following provisions of this Act. Section 14(1) states: 'The immunities and privileges conferred by this part of this Act apply to any foreign or Commonwealth state other than the United Kingdom; and references to a state include reference to—(a) the sovereign or other Head of that State in his public capacity"; section 20(1) of the 1978 Act applies the Diplomatic Privileges Act 1964 to "a sovereign or other Head of State." The latter Act gives effect in English law to the Vienna Convention, Article 29 of which provides: "The person of a diplomatic agent shall be inviolable. He shall not be liable to any form of arrest or detention. The receiving state shall treat him with due respect and shall take all appropriate steps to prevent any attack on his person, freedom or dignity." Article 39 of the Convention taken together with section 20(1) of the 1978 Act constitutes the core argument of Mr Clive Nicholls, QC, for the General:

1. Every person entitled to privileges and immunities shall enjoy them from the moment he enters the territory of the receiving state on proceeding to take up his post or, if already in its territory, from the moment when his appointment is notified to the Ministry for Foreign Affairs or such other ministry as may be agreed.

Then the following crucial passage:

2. When the functions of a person enjoying privileges and immunities have come to an end, such privileges and immunities shall normally cease at the moment when he leaves the country, or on expiry of a reasonable period in which to do so, but shall subsist until that time, even in case of armed conflict.

However, with respect to acts performed by such a person in the exercise of his functions as a member of the mission immunity shall continue to subsist.

Counsel for the general argued that section 20(1) of the 1978 Act taken together with Article 39 confers the same immunity on a Head of State or a former Head of State as on a head or former head of a diplomatic mission; that after a Head of State ceases to be such he ceases to enjoy any immunity in respect of personal or private acts but continues to enjoy immunity in respect of public acts performed by him as Head of State in the exercise by him of sovereign power in that capacity; and that therefore the conduct alleged against him in the second international warrant of arrest related not to his private or personal conduct but to his conduct when exercising sovereign power as Head of State of the Republic of Chile.

Counsel for the applicant government argued that crimes of the magnitude of those of which Pinochet was accused could not be considered part of his sovereign functions as Head of State. In support of this he pointed to various charters and statutes which set up international tribunals for the punishment of crimes against humanity and the fact that under such provisions Heads of State were quite specifically not exempted. But the court distinguished between those internationally agreed tribunals and extradition, and held that they did not violate the principle that one sovereign state will not impede another in relation to its sovereign acts.

The final ruling of the court, delivered in the judgment of the Lord Chief Justice was this: "I would for my part accordingly hold that the applicant is entitled to immunity as a former sovereign from the criminal and civil process of the English courts." Leave being given, an appeal to the House of Lords then followed.

The case was heard in the House of Lords on November 25, 1998. This particular hearing was subsequently nullified on the grounds that one of their Lordships, Lord Hoffman, failed to disclose his relationship with Amnesty International, an intervening party in the case. There was no suggestion that Lord Hoffman, a greatly respected judge, was or even might have been biased in any way. Merely that he had failed to make a disclosure which ought to have been made. Nevertheless it is important to consider, quite briefly, what the remaining four Law Lords said.

Lord Slynn of Hadley neatly encapsulated the issue before the House:

> "The sole question is whether he is entitled to immunity as a former Head of State from arrest and extradition proceedings in the United Kingdom in respect of acts alleged to have been committed whilst he was Head of State."

His Lordship then reviewed the background events leading to the arrest, the arguments put before the Divisional Court and the reasons for the conclusions which that court reached. His own view was that immunity continued to exist; that the developing law regarding international tribunals had not variated or cut back that immunity, and that

> "the fact that in carrying out other functions a Head of State commits an illegal act does not mean that he is no longer to be regarded as carrying out one of his functions. If it did, the immunity in respect of criminal acts would be deprived of much of its content. I do not think it right to draw a distinction for this purpose between acts whose criminality and moral obliquity is more or less great."

Lord Lloyd of Berwick took a similar view. Among the most significant *dicta* in Lord Lloyd's judgment were: "Where a person is accused of organizing the commission of crimes as the head of the government, in co-operation with other governments, and carrying out those crimes through the agency of the police and the secret service, the inevitable conclusion must be that he was acting in a sovereign capacity and not in a personal or private capacity"; "The setting up of these special international tribunals for the trial of those accused of genocide and other crimes against humanity, including torture, shows that such crimes, when committed by heads of state or other responsible government officials cannot be tried in the ordinary courts of other states. If they could, there would be little need for the international tribunal"; "In my view the immunities which Senator Pinochet is entitled to under section 20 of the State Immunity Act are identical to the immunities which he enjoys at common law."

Lords Nicholls, Steyn and Hoffman took a contrary view. Rejecting the argument for immunity Lord Nicholls said, "In the same way as acts of torture and hostage-taking stand outside the limited immunity afforded to a former Head of State by section 20 because those acts cannot be regarded by international law as a function of a Head of State, so for a similar reason Senator Pinochet cannot bring himself within any such broad principle applicable to state officials." Lord Nicholls concluded: "I would allow this appeal. It cannot be too plainly stated that the acts of torture and hostage-taking with which Senator Pinochet is charged are offences under United Kingdom statute law. This country has taken extra-territorial jurisdiction for these crimes. The sole question before your Lordships is whether, by reason of his status as a former Head of State, Senator Pinochet is immune from the criminal processes of this country, of which extradition forms a part. Arguments about the effect on this country's diplomatic relations with Chile if extradition were allowed to proceed, or with Spain if refused, are not matters for the court. These are, *par excellence,* political matters for consideration by the Secretary of State in the exercise of his discretion under section 12 of the Extradition Act."

Lord Steyn's judgment was that the acts alleged against Senator Pinochet could not be regarded as official acts of state in the light of the present state of international law: "The normative principles of international law do not require that such high crimes should be classified as acts performed in the exercise of the functions as Head of State." Lord Hoffman agreed.

This ruling of the Lords by a majority of three to two created a sensation. The Court of Appeal had been unanimous, and while majority decisions in the House of Lords were not uncommon, such a sharp division of opinion by the highest judges in the land upon so internationally significant an issue had far-reaching implications.

The Times declared the judgment a "watershed ruling for human rights." In an article by the diplomatic editor the view was expressed, with good reason, that the ruling would have an immediate and widespread influence on international law, marking a watershed in attempts to bring to justice those accused of human rights' violations. From now on there would be no hiding place for dictators, and leaders with blood on their hands would think twice before travelling to Britain and much of Western Europe. Amnesty International, on a somewhat triumphalist note, declared: "It is a ground-breaking acknowledgement of the principle of universal jurisdiction for crimes against humanity, and of the international obligation to co-operate in the investigation and trial of those accused of such crimes." Amnesty said that the ruling, which had been made two weeks before the 50th anniversary of the Universal Declaration of Human Rights, reaffirmed the international community's commitment towards the fulfilment of basic human rights for all. However, *The Times* correspondent very sensibly sounded a note of caution by pointing out the potential conflict between the human rights factor and the well-established principle that a state does not and should not adjudicate upon events which are the internal affairs of another state. In Chile itself the ruling caused considerable civil disturbance between supporters and opponents of Pinochet, and the Chilean Social Democratic government expressed the deepest concern that a former of Head of State should be arrested and made subject to English legal process for actions for which he had already been granted immunity in his own country. *The Times* leader of November 26 very lucidly summed up the current position:

> "The precedent set is that crimes under international law can both override the doctrines of sovereign immunity, and that national courts can, in these cases, claim universality of jurisdiction."

The headnote in *The Times* law report of November 26 encapsulated the ratio of the Lords decision:

> "A former Head of State enjoys immunity from arrest and extradition proceedings in the United Kingdom only in respect of official acts performed in the exercise of his functions as Head of State. The crimes of torture and hostage-taking could not be regarded as part of the functions of a Head of State."

Meanwhile the political situation arising from the case was becoming more tense. A Chilean government delegation, led by Jose Miguel Insulza, the Foreign Minister, arrived in London to request the Home Secretary to intervene to prevent the extradition of General Pinochet to Spain.

President Frei of Chile said that the British authorities should respect Chilean extra-territoriality laws and that Chile would continue to argue the case that General Pinochet was protected by immunity. The President maintained that Spain had no authority to pass judgment upon crimes committed in Chile.

Meanwhile General Pinochet, who had been operated on in the London Clinic was moved to the Grovelands Priory Hospital, North London. At 83 he had made a remarkable recovery from the spinal surgery he had received but it was now said by the medical authorities that he was undergoing assessment for stress and stress-related disorders and that he was under the care of the distinguished psychiatrist Geoffrey Lloyd, the medical director of the Grovelands Priory. A Home Office spokesman confirmed that under the 1989 Extradition Act the Home Secretary can refuse extradition on compassionate grounds if a person is considered unfit to stand trial for health reasons. Baroness Thatcher was quoted as saying, "The Senator is old, frail and sick, and on compassionate grounds alone should be allowed to return to Chile." This proposal, however, raised the question of what the position of the senator would be if he were allowed to return to his own country. Although the Chilean Foreign Minister said the former dictator would face justice if allowed to return home authorities in Santiago told a different story. Key figures in the judiciary, the military and both government and opposition made it clear that retirement into private life was the worst that the general might anticipate. He had been guaranteed immunity on the basis of the vastly improved state of the nation at the end of his rule, and that was that.

The final decision in extradition lies not with the court but with the Home Secretary and the developing situation was creating the gravest of dilemmas for Mr Jack Straw and the British Government. To return the General to Chile on the understanding that he would face some sort of trial in that country would be an obvious fudge. On the other hand to order extradition would have grave consequences for Anglo-Chilean relations. Here the economic as well as the political factor was a serious consideration. Britain's exports to Chile in 1997 totalled £210.5 million and major British companies such as BAT, the tobacco and finance firm, Unilever, the food and household products company, Coats Viyella and Royal and Sun Alliance had substantial investments in that country. It could also be said that an impartial trial in Spain would be most unlikely, and in any event the evidence would be available in Chile and not in Spain. It was further suggested that there was an element of hypocrisy on the part of Spain since those who participated in the brutal suppression of opposition by the Franco regime or indeed the excesses of the earlier Marxist Government which resulted in Franco's actions in the first place, have never been put on trial.

The proposal that Pinochet should be tried in this country was never realistic. First, the evidence would be difficult to obtain and hence a conviction most unlikely. Secondly, the element of interference in the internal affairs of another country would be painfully blatant.

A further cause for concern was the strain which the divisive effect of these events was placing on the young democracy in Chile. The army, although accepting civilian rule, still occupies a powerful position in the political structure. It enjoys a reserved set of seats in the Senate and an index-linked budget. Moreover the opposition parties consist of the centre right National Renewal Party and the Independent Democratic Union whose programme has strong overtones of the Pinochet regime when the General was in power. The roots of democracy in Chile are set in shallow soil which could easily be disturbed. The division of opinion about the future of General Pinochet could lead to a new polarisation.

Meanwhile the subject of all this confusion and concern had been declared fit to leave hospital and attend court. From Grovelands Priory the General and his entourage travelled to Lindale Close on the Wentworth

Estate in Virginia Water, an exclusive private estate where a house had been rented by the Chilean government for his occupation. The 1,750 acre estate, whose residents include famous personalities, is sited in a heavily wooded area, security being the responsibility of the Surrey and Metropolitan police.

The decision of the Home Secretary as to whether to uphold or discharge my warrant was awaited with considerable concern. The Home Office had announced that no advance notice of his decision would be given, and lawyers for Amnesty International and other human rights groups were worried that should Mr Straw's decision go in his favour, the general could be rushed to his waiting plane at Brize Norton before the Home Secretary's decision could be challenged in the High Court. The Home Secretary's choices were stark. If he ordered extradition to proceed he would alienate a friendly state with which the United Kingdom had important trading relations. If he took a course which enabled Pinochet to return to Chile he would provoke outrage among a great many people, including those of his own party. In the event the Home Secretary signed the authority to proceed with extradition. He set out his reasons in a letter which was sent to all the parties concerned. That statement summarised the basic principles embodied in the European Convention and the Extradition Act 1989 and affirmed that the Home Secretary could find no convincing reason as to why he should not apply those principles in this particular case. It was clear, however, that on the issue of immunity he had been strongly influenced by the House of Lords ruling.

Then came another bombshell. Lord Lamont and Mr Howarth, MP had criticised Lord Hoffman for failing to declare an interest when sitting on the case in the Lords. Amnesty International was an intervening body in the hearing and Lord Hoffman had been an unpaid director of Amnesty International Charity Ltd, an affiliated group. It was also the case that Lady Hoffman was an administrative assistant at Amnesty. It was Lord Hoffman's casting vote that sealed the Law Lords three to two decision that the former dictator did not enjoy immunity from extradition proceedings.

Lawyers for General Pinochet then petitioned the Lords for a ruling that Lord Hoffman's judgment be set aside. The five who sat to hear the petition were Lords Browne-Wilkinson, Hutton, Hope, Goff and Nolan. Their decision was that Lord Hoffman should indeed have declared his interest. Consequently, with the exclusion of his judgment the House had been evenly divided and the issue of General Pinochet's immunity would have to be tried again.

At the renewed hearing the question arose, for the first time, whether any of the alleged offences had occurred before General Pinochet had been recognised by this country as Head of State.

The second judgment of the House of Lords was delivered on March 24, 1999. This time there were seven Law Lords; Lords Browne-Wilkinson, Goff of Chieveley, Hope of Craighead, Hutton, Saville of Newdigate, Millett and Phillips of Worth Matravers. This time a new element was introduced, namely the Convention against Torture and other Cruel, Inhuman or Degrading Treatment or Punishment 1984. The court held, by a majority of five to two, that a former Head of State of a country which had ratified the Convention had no immunity from extradition from the United Kingdom to a third country for acts of torture committed in his own country while he was Head of State after the date when the Convention came into effect in all three countries. For an offence to be extraditable under Section 2 of the Extradition Act 1989 it must have been a criminal offence punishable under English law at the time it was allegedly committed. As acts of torture committed extraterritorially did not become punishable under English law until section 134 of the Criminal Justice Act 1984 came into effect on September 29, 1988, acts of torture committed outside the requesting state prior to that date were not extraditable.

Following this ruling, which effectively reduced the remaining outstanding charges to three, the Home Secretary signed a second authority to proceed. He gave a statement of his reasons to all interested parties. At the request of the Spanish Government I signed a further warrant and once again the issue was before the courts.

Postscript

The eventual outcome was that Pinochet was released on grounds of ill-health, and returned to Chile where Judge Juan Guzmán Tapia ruled he was fit to stand trial and put him under house arrest. By the time of his death (10 December 2006), some 300 criminal charges were still pending against him there for human rights abuses, tax evasion and embezzlement. He stood accused of corruptly obtaining some $28 million.

CHAPTER 13

Summing It Up

In the course of this work I have dwelt sometimes upon the comic, sometimes the tragic and occasionally on the academic side of my professional life. When I ask myself what conclusions may be drawn in order to contribute some useful suggestions for the future better administration of criminal justice I am driven to the doleful conviction that the answer must be: very few indeed. This I fully realise, will be considered a negative and unconstructive approach compared with the thought and ingenuity which has been injected into the subject of crime and punishment in recent years. One Home Secretary after another has been under pressure from the public to do something about crime. In the 1920s and 1930s crime was, of course, as always a matter of public concern. It was not, however, a political football as it is today.

I recall one General Election some years ago at which the Opposition shadow Home Secretary declared that under the incumbent government the incidence of rape had increased. The absurdity of such a claim needs no further comment. Governments today are obliged to place reduction in the crime figures alongside other policy points such as improvement in the unemployment position, control of inflation and better quality education, health treatment and housing. The result of this pressure has been a series of Acts of Parliament designed to introduce new methods of combating crime by strengthening the police service, increasing police powers and those of the courts, and devising new forms of community penalties. Far be it from me to criticise these initiatives. New solutions must always be sought for old problems in society, but it has to be admitted that the impact all this has made on the incidence of crime has been disappointing to say the least. The figures for various types of offence have fluctuated over the years and officialdom presents the statistics in the best possible light. I feel it strange to have to inform a defendant that only half the sentence I have passed will be served. I cannot see why supervision on release should not be something quite separate from the sentence itself. The same question could be asked about parole and remission. Should a prisoner incarcerated for a grave crime expect early release for behaving himself in prison, or should he anticipate a later release for misbehaviour?

Thus the perennial question remains: forward to more sophisticated sentencing or back to basics. Since neither policy has made any appreciable impact on the criminal statistics of our nation, this author would not presume to attempt an answer to this question. The most I would seek to do would be to make a few observations on the basis of a lifetime spent in the criminal courts.

I believe that stipendiary magistrates—shortly to be redesignated district judges (magistrates' courts)—possess a greater insight into the practical day-to-day problems of crime and punishment than any other branch of the judiciary. I think therefore that their views should always be canvassed on matters relating to sentencing. I also believe that bodies set up to consider and advise upon this subject should always contain a member of the stipendiary bench. In this context I would emphasise the term "practical experience."

Once or twice in the course of my career I have attended courses organized by university departments of criminology. Most of the lectures and discussions turned upon criminal statistics, the methods by which they are gathered and the conclusions which can be drawn from a study of them. I have no doubt there is a place for crime in society as an academic study, but I must admit that I heard little which had much bearing on my work on the bench.

When I was first appointed a stipendiary the then Chief Magistrate, Sir Frank Milton, gave me some sound advice. He said that the work I was about to undertake was a very "hit and miss" affair, and that the most one could achieve was to keep some sort of order. How very true that is. Crime can only be contained and discouraged. It cannot, even on a limited scale, be suppressed. The present (1999) Government's policy was stated in the expression: "Tough on crime, tough on the causes of crime." Nobody could reasonably quarrel with the sentiments expressed in this maxim, but what are the causes of crime? The question is as old as the human race, and so are many of the causes.

I was once asked at a dinner party whether I believed in original sin. My reply was that this is a doctrine for which I consider the evidence to be overwhelming. One does not need to read the *Bible* to be convinced of this—only the newspapers. I have always believed, and still do, in the validity of absolute values. I also believe that morality, like liberty, is indivisible. I am further convinced that the root cause of crime lies in human nature and not the defects of society—though these may contribute. There is no conclusive dividing line between what we call sin on the one hand and crime on the other. The only distinction is one of labels. The latter is that form of evil or immoral conduct which impinges on the public sector, while the former does not. The distinction is by no means one of gravity. To steal a man's wife may have far more serious consequences than to steal his watch, yet the latter is a criminal offence while the former is not.

The great Dr Johnson lived in the 18th century. This was the period of the so-called Enlightenment—a philosophical optimism about the nature of man which proclaimed his natural rationality and goodness as opposed to the biblical teaching. Johnson saw this a sheer romantic nonsense. "Mankind" he wrote "are universally corrupt, but corrupt in different degrees; as they are universally ignorant, yet with greater or less irradiations of knowledge." But Johnson would not have seen this as a case for despair since a sickness can only be tackled after an accurate diagnosis has been made. But these are matters for churchmen, not politicians.

Can government do much about the external causes of crime? Probably the answer is: not a great deal. Youth training schemes help to alleviate the boredom of unemployment which is a factor in youth crime, but there are other, more subtle influences in life today which are less amenable to administrative solutions. Notwithstanding great material progress and the advancement in the standard of living of the great majority, there seems to be widespread insecurity. This is not only insecurity of work but insecurity of mind and spirit. In today's world nothing seems made to last, as once it was. In everything from marriages and human relationships to jobs and homes there seems everywhere to be a lack of permanence and an absence of commitment. This environment undermines stability and long-term purpose. Quietude of mind and soul become increasingly difficult when on film and television ever greater violence is produced lest the viewer is developing a dangerous immunity. The drug culture is only one area which seeks to satisfy the craving for emotional "highs." Under the synthetic jollity of the modern age there is despair. Suicide has been identified as the second biggest cause of death among young men. There are fruitful fields here for the churches, but even among them the influence of relativist morality is creeping in.

Yet I do not wish to conclude this book on a dismal note. Nor do I need to. Man is no angel but neither is he a devil. Young people who run into trouble with the law grow into responsible citizens. Most offenders are once only, and one appearance in court deters for good. People with long criminal records go straight in the end, and under the right kind of supervision many wrongdoers change their ways. Crime is incurable, but criminals are not. I very much hope that in my long career on the bench I may have contributed to this. One offender reformed is worth a dozen punished.

And there, with a final expression of gratitude to my reader for having shared my thoughts, ideas and memories thus far, I lay down my pen.

Appendix

BUCKINGHAM PALACE

17th May, 2001

Dear Mr. Bartle,

Thank you for your letter of 10th May with which you enclosed a copy of your book entitled "Bow Street Beak" - an account of the twenty years which you spent on the Stipendiary Bench of the Court, which included the memorable case of Michael Fagan and his unscheduled visits to Buckingham Palace.

Your book has been shown to The Queen, who has asked that her sincere thanks be conveyed to you for your thoughtfulness in sending it. Her Majesty was interested to read your reminiscences, and has directed that the copy be held in the Royal Library at Windsor.

Yours sincerely,

MRS. DEBORAH BEAN
Chief Correspondence Officer

Ronald Bartle, Esq.

Bow Street Beak

Index

A

absconding *116*
abuse of process *51, 61, 67*
access to justice *103*
actual bodily harm *128*
actus reus *149*
addiction *52*
adjournments *123*
advance disclosure *148*
adversarial trial *156*
advocacy *105, 121, 126*
affirmation *142*
aggression *26, 46*
Aids *55*
alcohol *26, 46, 53*
alternatives to imprisonment *45, 149*
amateurs *95*
Amnesty International *173, 175*
animals *29*
appeal *31, 32, 54, 64, 66, 76, 87, 99, 141, 172*
Armstrong, Patrick *64*
arrest *168*
assassination *79*
assault *46*
  assaults on police *47*
  indecent assault *51*
assignment of lawyers *124*

Assizes *99, 124*
Atomic Bomb Memorial Museum *163*
atrocities *165*
Attorney General *76*
Attwell, Vernon *63*
Avon and Somerset Constabulary *64*

B

bad argument *126*
Badge, Peter *112*
bail *21, 115*
  bail in Japan *159*
  presumption of bail *115*
Bangladeshis *133*
Bank of Credit and Commerce International *88*
Bank of England *89*
Bar Council *141*
Barraclough, Kenneth *109*
barristers *105, 121*
Bartle, George (father) *132*
Bartle, George (grandfather) *131*
begging *26*
being caught *37*
Belmarsh Prison *80–81*
Best, George *46*
bias *76, 108, 173*
binding-over *29, 50, 95*

Birmingham Six *75*
Black Committee *150*
Black Death *94*
Blitz *133*, *136*
Bloomsbury *105*
Blundell, Robert *108*
"Bomber" Harris statue *80*
Bow Street *97*, *110*, *115*
   Bow Street Magistrates' Court *11*
   Bow Street Runners *12*
boxing *135*
breaking windows *38*
bribery *13*, *59*
briefs *138*
Brixton Prison *20*
Brock, Det Supt. *65*
Brooks's Club *33*
Browne-Wilkinson, Lord *179*
brutality *59*
Bryant, Det Insp *65*
Buckingham Palace *17–24*
   "Buckingham Palace assault" *50*
   "palace defendants" *23*
   security *18*, *20*
Buddhism *153*
bureaucratic thinking *141*
Burge, James *138*
burglary *20*
buskers *30–31*
Buster the dog *29*
Buzzard, John Huxley *137*

C

Caesar's Palace *23*
call to the Bar *136*
Cambridge *135*, *137*
Camelot *35*
Campaign Against Drink Driving *39*
cannabis *53–57*
Cannon Row Police Station *20*
Carter, Sarah Jane *18*
casinos *35*
cautioning *25*, *149*
chambers *138*
character *42*
Chelsea *108*
Chief Metropolitan Magistrate *15*, *98*, *100*, *141*
children *139*
   child abuse *51*
   Children and Young Persons Act 1963 *48*
Chile *165*
"China Town" *48*
civil rights *105*
civil servants *27*
Clarke, Kenneth *76*
clergy *131–134*
Clerkenwell *107*
clerks *39*, *117*
   barrister's clerk *138*
clubs *33*
cocaine *56*, *89*
cockroaches *33*
Cohen, Lord *136*
Columbia *89*
combination order *45*
committal proceedings *146–147*
common sense *45*, *127*, *140*
Commonwealth *85*

community sentences *42, 128, 149, 181*
compassion *36, 107, 111, 176*
competence *106*
complexity *103*
Computer Misuse Act *87, 88*
conditional discharge *28, 47, 53*
confessions *63, 146*
confidence
    public confidence *48*
confiscation *24*
consistency *42*
conspiracy *89–90*
containment *58, 182*
contrition *37*
Convention against Torture, etc. *179*
Coral Racing Ltd *35*
corroboration *146*
corruption *59, 67, 97, 183*
Costa del Sol *91*
costs *34, 36, 103, 122, 148*
court clerks. See *clerks*
Court of Appeal *32, 47, 65, 73, 77, 174*
Covent Garden *11, 30*
crack cocaine *53*
crime *39–58*
    a matter of choice *53*
    causes of crime *183*
    containment of crime *54, 184*
    crime reduction *181*
    crimes against humanity *165, 172*
    human tragedy of crime *125*
    international crime *83, 86*
    tough on crime, etc. *182*
Criminal Justice Act 1984 *179*
Criminal Justice Act 1991 *43*

Criminal Law Act 1977 *148*
criminology *41, 182*
Cromwell, Oliver *18*
cross-examination *127*
Crown Court *41, 51, 99, 102, 109, 147*
Crown Prosecution Service *61, 121*
cruelty *38*
culpability *41*
Cumberland Lodge *126*
custody *47*
cynicism *148*

D

Davies, Tom *107*
death
    death penalty *85*
    death threats *37*
decriminalisation *54*
defence *124*
delay *61, 102*
democracy *80, 177*
    democratic ideal *52*
demonstrations *39*
deportation *24*
Desert Rats *135*
detachment *122*
deterrence *41, 184*
Detmold *135*
De Veil, Thomas *12*
diplomacy *119*
    Diplomatic Privileges Act 1964 *171*
directives *42*
Director of Public Prosecutions *61, 66, 111*
disadvantage *105*

189

discharges 46
discontinued cases 124
discretion 34
dishonesty 46
disorder 94
disqualification
  from driving 39
district judge 11
dock brief 124
doctor
  fake doctor 28
domestic violence 38
Donaldson, John Sutherland 63
drink-driving 38, 39, 148
drugs 47, 52–58
  demand reduction 57
  drug culture 184
  drug-fuelled crime 53
  drug-trafficking 83
  Holland 55
  Home Office Advisory Council on the Misuse of Drugs 55
  World Ministerial Drugs Summit 57
drunkenness 25, 39, 115
due process 141
Duke of Newcastle 13
Dunne, Laurence 108
Durand, Victor QC 138

E

economy 141
ecstasy 53
Edinburgh 55
education 181
  Education Corps 135

effectiveness 141
efficiency 93, 140
"either way" offences 146–147
election for trial 147
Elephant and Castle 80
Elizabeth (Queen Elizabeth II) 17, 185
emotional problems 17
English language 127
Enlightenment 183
Epicureans 36
Erskine, Thomas 79
Essex 139
European Convention 85, 170, 178
Evans, Nicholas 168
evidence 120, 142
  rules of evidence 119
expedition of cases 103
experience 182
  life experience 106
extradition 12, 80, 83, 113, 117, 165
  Extradition Act 1870 84
  Extradition Act 1989 84, 168, 178
extra-judicial justice 151
extremists 80

F

Fagan, Michael 17–24
fairness 93, 109
fair trial 51, 61
false accounting 87
family background (of the author) 131–151
Faulkner, David 43
FBI 86
Ferley, Joyce 117

Fielding, Henry *12*
Fielding, John *12*, *116*
fines *24*, *28*, *39*, *48*
    fine default *149*
firearms *79*
firmness *111*
fledgling lawyers *105*, *125*
food hygiene *33*
football hooligans *47*
forgery *87*
fraud *81*, *83*, *89*, *137*, *180*
freedom *80*
Frei, President (of Chile) *176*
French, Stanley *106*
fugitives *12*, *83*, *167*

G

gambling *34*, *126*
gaming *35*
gangsters *48*
Garland, Mr Justice *62*
Garrick Club *22*
genealogy *131*
genocide *166*
George III *79*
Gerrard Street *48*
Goff, Lord *179*
Golden Crescent *56*
Golden Triangle *56*
good behaviour *29*, *95*
Gordon Riots *13*
Goulden, Robert *138*
gravitas *107*, *108*
gravity *42*, *103*, *151*, *157*
Gray's Inn *111*, *136*

Great Marlborough Street *115*
Grierson, Edward *95*
grievous bodily harm *48*, *128*
Grovelands Priory Hospital *176*
guidelines *42*
Guildford Four *63*
guitar *31*

H

habeas corpus *170*
hacking *86*, *88*
Hadfield, James *79*
Hall, Marshall *30*
Hastings, Patrick *136*
Hattersley, Roy *29*
Hawksmoor, Nicholas *132*
Hayes, Brian *67*
health *25*
    health hazard *33*
hearsay *87*
heroin *56*
High Court *32*, *76*
Hiroshima *160*
Hitler, Adolph *80*
Hoffman, Lord *87*, *173*, *178*
holocaust *166*
Home, Lord *108*
Home Office *141*
Home Secretary *20*, *65*, *76*, *86*, *98*, *176*, *181*
homosexual solicitation *50*
honesty *153*
Hope, Lord *179*
Hopkin, Daniel *112*
Hopkin, David *111*
Hornton Street *138*

hotels *33*
"hot pursuit" *84*
House of Commons *20, 80, 138*
House of Lords *87, 172*
Howarth, Mr MP *178*
Huguenot refugees *132*
humanity *36*
   crimes against humanity *165, 172*
   human folly *35*
   human nature *183*
   human rights *175*
   human weakness *38*
humility *116*
humour *112*
Hutchinson, Jeremy (Lord) *138*
Hutton, Lord *179*
hypocrisy *177*

I

imprisonment *46, 126*
   suspended sentence *42*
improvements *140*
indecent exposure *49*
Inner Temple *136*
innocence
   presumption of innocence *67*
Inns of Court *136*
   Inns of Court Regiment *110*
   Inns of Court School of Law *126*
insanity *79*
instructions *127*
Insulza, Jose Miguel *176*
interference with the course of justice *116*
International Court *135*

international law *165*
investigation *157*
IRA *79–80*
Irvine, Lord *103*
Islington North constituency *137*
Italy *22*

J

Jak (cartoonist) *34*
James Committee *148*
Japan *153–164*
Jena University *131*
Jennings, Robert *135*
Jesus College *135*
Jews *133*
Johnson, Dr *183*
Jones, Alun QC *87*
judge
   circuit judge *100*
   imprisonment of *39*
judicial independence *42, 75*
judicial review *170*
Judicial Studies Board *112*
jurisdiction *11, 146, 166*
jury *123, 147*
   right to trial by jury *148*
justice *11*
   Justices' Clerks' Society *141*
   Justices of the Peace Act 1361 *94*
   summary justice *12*
juveniles *48, 150*

K

keepers of the peace *94*
kerb crawling *49*

Kidotai 155
knighthood *13, 100*
Knight, Ronnie *91*
knowledge *117*
Kurata, Seiji *156*
Kyoto *153*

L

Labour Party *29, 93, 137*
Ladbrooke Racing (Central London) Ltd *35*
Lambeth *106*
    Bishop of Lambeth *145*
Lamont, Lord *178*
laughter in court *25–38*
"laundering" *83, 89*
Lauterpacht, Professor *135*
law
    law and order *13*
    Law Lords *173*
    Law Society *112, 141*
Lawson, Edmund QC *67*
lawyers *13*
Leatherhead *134*
Leeds University *103*
Leicester Square *30–31*
leniency *39, 42, 47*
Levin, Vladimir *86*
liberty *143*
lies *144*
life imprisonment *64*
Lincoln, Samuel *138*
Lincoln's Inn *136*
Lisle Street *48*
Lloyd, Geoffrey *176*

Lloyd-Hughes, D Ch Supt. *21*
Lloyd, Lord *173*
London Clinic *168*
London Government Act 1963 *32*
Lord Chancellor *11, 34, 75, 94, 101, 115*
Lord Chief Justice *39, 45, 53, 66, 101, 170, 172*
loss *37*
Lotteries and Amusements Act 1976 *35*
Luton and Dunstable *28*

M

Mackay, Lord *76*
Mackinon, Neil QC *137*
mafia *80*
magistrates *93–104*
    lay justices *93*
    Magistrates' Association *42, 99, 104, 113, 141, 145*
    "police magistrate" *97*
    selection of *99*
Major, John *80*
make-believe bishop *27*
manipulation *61, 74*
Mary Ward Settlement *105*
mayhem *13*
Mayhew, Patrick *76*
media/press *13, 49, 66, 76*
medical reports *53*
mens rea *149*
mental health/impairment *27, 150*
mercy *116*
Metropolitan Police Courts Act 1839 *15, 98*
MI6 *91*

Middlesex *12*, *97*
Middle Temple *136*
military junta *167*
Miller, James *23*
Milton, Frank *109*, *182*
Ministry of Justice *11*
"misfits" *116*
mitigation *42*, *109*, *125*
money *25*
Monte Carlo *35*
morale *100*
morality *52*, *183*
Mortimer, John *124*
Mountbatten, Lord *79*
mouse droppings *33*
Mullin, Chris *75*
murder *48*
  murder of a judge *80*
Murdoch, Rupert *60*

N

Nadeem, Maurice *21*
Nadir, Azil *91*
Nagasaki *160*
narcotics *56*
National Lottery *36*
National Service *134*
Neighbourhood Watch *81*
News International *60*
Nicholls, Clive QC *171*
no case to answer *148*
Northamptonshire Police *60*
nuisance *25*
Nuremberg Tribunal *166*

O

oath *142*
  judicial oath *39*
  Oaths Act 1978 *142*
obscene publications *52*
obsession *37*
Official Secrets Act *91*
Old Bailey *17*, *19*, *42*, *65*, *79*
Old Etonian *108*
Old Street *107*
Orwell, George *132*
Osaka *154*

P

Paris *89*
Parkinson, Edward Graham *113*
Parliamentary All-Party Penal Affairs Group *150*
parole *182*
"peep shows" *52*
Pentagon *88*
Percival, Spencer *79*
perjury *60*, *145*
Peterloo Massacre *97*
philosophy *36*
Piccadilly Circus *31*
pickpockets *22*
pigeons *28*
pillars of society *117*
Pinochet Ugarte, General Augusto *165*
"planting" *59*
Playboy *25*
police *12*, *19*, *24*, *26*, *59–77*, *93*, *151*, *178*, *181*
  armed police *155*
  impersonating *27*

Index

in the dock *59*
Japanese police *154*
Police and Criminal Evidence Act 1984 *87*
River Police *140*
political or military offences *85*
politics *137*, *181*
Polly Peck *91*
pomposity *127*
Poor Persons cases *105*, *108*
pornography *107*
  child pornography *123*
Powell, Frank *107*
preachers *30*
prejudice *39*, *61*, *116*
presentation *127*
pre-sentence reports *37*, *53*, *128*
previous convictions *43*, *148*
Princess Anne *79*
probation *47*, *126*, *128*, *149*
procedure *141*
Proll, Astrid *110*
prostitutes *36*, *115*
psychology *17*
psychotropic plants *56*
public health *33*
public service *94*
pupillage *137*

Q

Quarter Sessions *99*, *124*
Queen's Bench *62*

R

"**Raymond**" *88*

realism *148*
reasons *51*, *129*
reconciliation *107*
Redhill *132*
reformation *41*, *47*, *184*
rejection *37*
  rejection of advances *50*
relationships *25*
release *182*
religion *144*, *153*
remission *182*
remorse *37*
reputation *143*
respect *149*
responsibility *41*
restaurants *33*
retribution *41*, *117*
Ritsumeikan University *154*
"**road rage**" *46*
Robert, PC *19*
Rome Statute *166*
Rose, Geoffrey *106*
Royal Commissions *99*, *100*, *140*, *146*
Royal Opera House *25*
Rozenburg, Joshua *98*
RSPCA *28*
rule of law *52*
Runciman, Viscount *100*
Russell, Evelyn *110*, *140*
Rwanda *166*

S

Salad Days *135*
schooldays *132*
Scotland Yard *20*

Second World War *133*, *165*
security *18*, *20*, *79–82*, *178*
self-advancement *106*
self-advertisement *106*
sentencing *40*, *96*, *115*, *120*, *146*
    sentencing guidelines *42*
sex
    sex offences *49–50*
    sex shops *52*
Shaftesbury Avenue *48*
Sheiman, Lord Justice *32*
shooting *108*
shoplifting *37*, *40*, *50*
sin/original sin *183*
Skyrme, Thomas *139*
Slynn, Lord *173*
Smith, Sydney *97*
snake-charming *30*
social workers *128*
soft option *45*
Soho *12*, *48*
solemnity *25*
solicitors *105*, *112*, *121*, *138*
    duty solicitor *124*
sorrow *36*
Southport *131*
South West Court, Clapham *107*
sovereign immunity *170*
Spain *168*, *176*
Spitalfields, *132*
squares *31*
stability *184*
Staffordshire bull-terrier *29*
Stalin *163*
stalkers *37*

state immunity *167*
    State Immunity Act 1978 *171*
statistics *182*
Stevenson, Alan *108*
"sting" operation *91*
stipendiary magistrates *11*
    "flying stipes" *103*
    provincial stipendiaries *103*
St James's Park *29*
Stoics *36*
Stone's Justices' Manual *118*
streamlining procedure *146*
street
    street artists *30–31*
    street crime *54*, *154*
    street trading *40*, *115*
Sturge, Harold *107*
Style, Thomas Lionel *63*
suicide *184*
supervision *48*, *184*
Supreme Court Act 1981 *100*
sureties *115*
Surrey Constabulary *63*
suspended sentence *45*
    "Sword of Damocles" *45*, *149*

T

taking and driving away *128*
Taylor, Lord *45*
Taylor, Neil QC *137*
technicalities *84*
technology *83*
terrorism *80*, *83*
Thames Court *115*, *140*
Thatcher, Margaret *57*, *79*, *136*, *168*, *176*

theft *13, 21, 87, 125, 156*
third world *56*
Thomas, Professor D A *41*
Tokyo *84, 154, 166*
   Tokyo Convention *166*
Tomlinson, Richard *91*
tourists *50*
"trading" justices *13*
tragedy *25*
training *99*
tramps *26*
transfer for trial *147*
transvestites *49*
treason *79*
Treasury counsel *137*
trespass *21*
Triads *48*
Trooping the Colour *79*
trouble *25*
trust
   position of trust *125*
truth *156*
tyranny *97*

U

under-cover agents *90*
unemployment *181*
United Nations *83*
United Nations Asia and Far East Institute for the Prevention of Crime and the Treatment of Offenders *84*
United States of America *86*
unit fines *43*

V

vagrancy *25, 38*
victims *81, 125, 151*
Victoria (Queen Victoria) *11, 79*
Vienna Convention *171*
vigilantes *81*
vilification *77*
violence *13, 46–48, 60*

W

Walter Mitty *27*
Wapping *69, 140*
   Wapping riots *59*
warrants *32, 165*
Watkins, Lord Justice *62*
Welch, Saunders *12*
welfare *82*
West Africa *55*
West End *11, 115*
West London Court *108*
Westminster *11*
   Westminster City Council *32, 33*
Whitechapel *140*
Whitelaw, William *20*
White Papers *44*
Whybrow, Charles *19*
Widgery, Lord *39*
wildlife *28*
William Hill (London) Ltd *35*
wisdom *117, 128*
Woolwich *63*

Y

youth court *48*
youth training schemes *183*

Yugoslavia (former) *166*

Z
"zero tolerance" policing *149*

Three Cases that Shook the Law
by Ronald Bartle

There are cases in the annals of English criminal law that forever resonate. In *Three Cases that Shook the Law* former district judge Ronald Bartle has selected three for close scrutiny: cases where the defendants paid the ultimate penalty even though demonstrably the victims of injustice.

They are those of Edith Thompson who suffered due to her romantic mind-set, a young lover and the prevailing moral climate; William Joyce (Lord 'Haw Haw') where the law was stretched to its limits to accommodate treason; and Timothy Evans who died due to the lies of the principal prosecution witness Reginald John Halliday Christie who it later transpired was both a serial killer and the likely perpetrator.

Weaving narrative, transcripts and original court records the author presents the reader with a captivating book in which his long experience as a lawyer and on the bench is brought fully to bear.

'A cautionary tale which explores each case in fascinating detail via letters as well as transcripts and original court records. Criminal lawyers especially, as well as magistrates and judges will find it an illuminating read'
— Phillip Taylor MBE and Elizabeth Taylor of Richmond Green Chambers.

Paperback & ebook | ISBN 978-1-909976-30-6 | 2016 | 240 pages

www.WatersidePress.co.uk